YOUR BIZ YOUR WAY

LEARNING TO TRUST YOURSELF - RELAX! YOU'VE GOT THIS

JUDITH MORGAN

BUSTING THE BONKERSNESS

Published in 2017 by Judith Morgan

Copyright © 2017 Judith Morgan.

Judith Morgan has asserted her rights under the Copyright, Designs and Patents Act 1988 to be identified as the author of this work.

All rights reserved. No part of this publication may be reproduced, stored in a retrieval system, or transmitted in any form or by any means, electronic, mechanical, photocopying, recording or otherwise, without the prior permission of the copyright owner.

ISBN: 978-1-5272-1416-3

DEDICATION

For my clients, past, present and future

Thank you for everything you teach me

I love you, I really do

I know you know this

YOUR BIZ YOUR WAY

1. HAVE I LEFT IT TOO LATE? 1
2. WHY DO I FEEL I MUST DO IT ALL MYSELF? 3
3. WHY AM I ALWAYS COMPELLED TO START A NEW NOTEBOOK? 6
4. WHY AM I PLAGUED BY APPARENTLY INSURMOUNTABLE OBSTACLES? 9
5. WHAT MAKES THE FOLLY OF MULTIPLE PROJECTS SO SEDUCTIVE? 12
6. HOW DO I DECIDE WHAT'S "REAL" WORK? 14
7. I'M UNSURE. WHAT CAN I DO AND FOR WHOM? 19
8. HOW DO I SAY NO WITHOUT OFFENDING? 22
9. WHY IS IT SO HARD TO HEAR MY OWN VOICE? 26
10. LOOK HOW GREAT *THEY* ARE. WHY ON EARTH WOULD I EVEN BOTHER TRYING? 30
11. WHY DOESN'T IT FEEL FAIR IF MY LIFE IS LOVELY? 32
12. WHAT IF IT DOESN'T GO TO PLAN AGAIN? 36
13. HOW CAN NICE GIRLS DO NASTY THINGS? 39
14. HOW CAN I STEP UP TO A BIGGER GAME WITHOUT FEELING EXPOSED? 42
15. HOW CAN I LESSEN THE FEELINGS OF UTTER CHAOS? 44
16. WHY WOULD ANYONE WANT TO BUY MY STUFF? 48
17. WILL MY EFFORTS RESULT IN MY BECOMING A BAG LADY? 50

18. WHY DO I LIVE IN ENDLESS FEAR?..52

19. COULDN'T I JUST HELP PEOPLE FOR FREE? 57

20. HOW CAN PITCHING FOR WORK BE EASIER? 60

21. WHAT'S THE BEST WAY TO DISCOUNT?...63

22. WHAT'S THE RIGHT PRICE FOR MY STUFF?..65

23. HOW DO YOU GO FROM FREE TO FEE?...68

24. WHAT'S THE BEST WAY TO ENFORCE MY TERMS? 70

25. WILL I EVER LEARN TO LOVE MARKETING AND SELLING?................................77

26. WHY DO I FEEL LIKE I AM BEING UNPROFESSIONAL IN GIVING AWAY ALL MY BEST WORK?..83

27. WHY IS IT TAKING ME SO LONG TO GET MY WEBSITE LIVE?................................85

28. HOW CAN I BE LOUD ENOUGH OR DIFFERENT ENOUGH TO GET NOTICED?.....88

29. MUST I BLOW MY OWN TRUMPET?..92

30. HOW DO I GET COMFY WITH SELF-PROMOTION? 94

31. HOW DO I ASK FOR THE BUSINESS?..99

32. WHO AM I TO...? 103

33. WHY IS THERE NO MONEY IN MY IDEAS YET?...105

34. IS IT OK TO TALK OPENLY ABOUT MY SPIRITUALITY?...107

35. WHAT ARE YOUR BEST TIPS FOR BETTER WORKING WITH MY BUSINESS PARTNER WHO IS ALSO MY HUSBAND, ESPECIALLY WHEN WE DON'T SEE EYE TO EYE?...111

36. WHY DO I ALWAYS PUT MY OWN SELF-CARE LAST?...116

37. WHY DO I FEEL BAD THAT MY WORK ISN'T EITHER HARD ENOUGH OR SUFFICIENTLY WORTHY OR INTELLECTUAL? 123

38. WHEN IS ENOUGH ENOUGH?...125

39. WHAT'S THE BEST WAY TO AVOID COMPROMISING MY FREEDOM?.............127

40. WHY DO I KEEP SELF-SABOTAGING AND SLOWING DOWN MY OWN PROGRESS?..129

41. IS THERE SOMETHING WRONG WITH ME? 133

42. WHY DO I FEEL INFERIOR TO BETTER QUALIFIED ARTISTS? 138

43. WHY DOES HAVING THE RIGHT MINDSET FEEL LIKE A BIT OF A GAME?.........142

44. IN EMERGENCIES, WHAT SHOULD I FOCUS ON?...147

45. WHEN IS IT OK TO BE BOTH A PERFECTIONIST AND A PROCRASTINATOR?.....152

46. WHY IS THERE SO MUCH WORK TO DO ALL THE TIME?...................................154

47. WHY DO I NOT HAVE CONTROL OF MY OWN DAY?...157

48. HOW DO WE RESPOND TO UNFAIR ONLINE REVIEWS? 162

49. HOW DO I DECIDE WHETHER AND WHEN TO EXPAND?...................................165

50. HOW MUCH TIME SHOULD I PUT INTO A NEW AREA OF BUSINESS OUTSIDE MY SWEET SPOT?...167

51. WHY AM I WAKING IN THE NIGHT WITH REMORSE AND TERRORS?...............169

52. WHY CAN'T I SUFFER FOOLS GLADLY? 172

FOREWORD

What do you most want to hear from me, I wonder?

I ask that because the genius of Judith's format in this book is that she knows exactly what you want to hear from her, and then she's answered you. Well, not 'you' precisely, of course, but people like you, and me.

In doing so, she's acting out a fundamental and often-forgotten principle of business at its best:

She's asked you what you need. What your problem is. And then she fulfils that need and solves that problem (by answering your question) in the unique inimitable way that is Judith.

If you were able to understand the problem of your audience as precisely and specifically as Judith does, then solve that problem in as unique, colourful and helpful way as Judith has, you'd be on your way to a cracking business.

So, back to my original question – what do you want to hear from me? I can't ask you. Like Judith has asked her clients. I'm not going to do any research (I'm Mr F**k It, do you think I do research?). So I have to guess.

And my guess is this. If you know anything about me (and I'm about to help you if you don't, too), and without blowing my own trumpet too forcefully (or maybe by placing a mute in my own trumpet, jazz style), I've been pretty successful in a variety of businesses, and in sharing the whole 'F**k It' thing with the world.

So you might be thinking that I wouldn't be asking these questions. But I am. My reading of the book has been accompanied by plenty of note-taking, a lot of 'I must remember that', some seriously useful insights into our current business situation and some frustrating reminders of things I thought I'd learnt but clearly forgotten.

So whether you're starting out, or you're an experienced entrepreneur, we keep asking many of these questions, and we're always grateful to hear the answers. Even if we've asked them before, and somehow forgotten the answers, like me.

I go to Judith when I need answers. And I often need answers. Sometimes I go to Judith when I need to understand the question actually.

And reading this has reminded me again why I do go to Judith. She is funny, direct, straight to the point and always insightful.

I don't know anyone like her. No one can answer my questions like she does.

And that, to swing back to my original point, is business at its best. Her doing her business her way. Helping me to do my business my way.

John C. Parkin
Author of the 'F**k It' books
Fano, Italy
20th November 2017

JOIN THE *ASK JUDITH* FACEBOOK GROUP TODAY

<u>www.22s.com/judith/askjudith</u>

Got a question about employing yourself for money and busting the bonkersness?

You don't need to wait until the publication of next year's book, or even until you have finished reading this one. You can ask your question today simply by joining the Ask Judith Facebook Group, open to all. I hope you'll come on over and join us even if you don't want to ask a question. We can talk about the issues raised in the book, you can share thoughts and comments and feedback with me, and everyone in the group can help and encourage you to run **Your Biz Your Way.**

HOW TO USE THIS BOOK

What's the best way to use this book?

If I were you, I'd read it all the way through first, hopefully in one sitting, or over a day or three. Mentally, or any which way, I'd bookmark or earmark the questions that speak to you particularly, as you go, with the intention of returning to them later.

There are 52 questions and that means you could use this as a yearbook if you wanted, tackling one a week, which would allow you plenty of time to think and feel through each question and notice which ones might require more thought or work than others. Whizz through the fast ones or even ignore those, knowing you have it cracked, and focus on the ones where you have a sense there's something in it for you.

Pop into the Ask Judith Facebook Group and discuss what you are learning about yourself and your biz, and ask for further clarification or talk it all through with me and the others in the group. ***www.22s.com/judith/askjudith***

Keep the book handy and remember where there are nuggets of gold in it for you, and pick it up every now and again expecting to find just what you need, just when you need it. Trust your intuition to know that for you.

A NOTE ABOUT *WEALTH DYNAMICS

In this book, I have referred to people occasionally by their Wealth Dynamics profile, such as Creator, Star and Mechanic. With an asterisk*.

Sometimes it is useful for me to know my clients' profiles, but it is by no means essential.

Bearing in mind what I say in the book about yet ANOTHER profiling system, and the opportunity to hide behind them or be limited by them, proceed with caution when I say that you can, if you wish, take your wealth profile test for $97 at http://www.yourwealthprofile.com

After you have received the results of your test, read the PDF - TWICE! Take your time.

Then pop into the Ask Judith Facebook group and those of us who know our profiles will share how they have helped us in our life and work.

But remember… I won't allow any hiding behind your profile. You have been warned.

ODD ONE OUT

"We start out knowing magic. We have shooting stars, cosmic universes, whirlwinds inside of us. But then it gets educated away."
Pam Grout, THANK & Grow Rich

My immediate family, the Morgans, are all employees. My father had two jobs, two careers really, and was quite the consummate employee. And he it was who gave me tips about how to be a good worker-bee and what to expect from a 9-5 when I started my first job in 1973.

My mother didn't work for money initially. Her job was to be my father's wife in his career in the Royal Marines; she was the Captain's, the Major's, the Colonel's lady and she very definitely had unpaid duties - entertaining, prizegiving, and looking after the soldiers' wives on overseas tours when their husbands were coming under gunfire and away from home and family themselves. After my Dad retired from his first career and my brother and I were teenagers still at boarding school and she'd done the housework by 9 a.m., my mother got her first proper paying job at forty years of age. My Dad wasn't all that keen on the idea; changes were afoot of which he didn't approve. There was one about the non-ironing of underpants, but that's another story for another day.

My brother worked for one bank for most of his career, rising from the lowliest of the low to the top of the tree and beyond, and all three of his children are, as I write, employees.

This made my decision to become firstly freelance and later properly self-employed somewhat odd.

The Morgans are employees.

Not so my wider family. On my father's side, there are at least four generations of employees, and his father was what was known in our family as a schoolmaster. But my two cousins on that side are both career self-employed pretty much and wide with it, as am I. I wouldn't say Del Boy was our role model but we recognise enough of DB in ourselves to laugh longer and harder than most. Proper entrepreneurs, like my cousins, can turn their hand to anything, whatever people want for money. It was ever thus and will ever be so. I seem to remember that it all began for my Welsh cousins with ice-cream, and then later mobile phones and for all I know, and suspect, by now they are probably into something else entirely. Whatever sells and whatever the market dictates. They will keep on their toes and abreast of the desires of their customers. Way to go, Boyos.

On my mother's side, her parents were farmers, and their parents were landlords at least towards the end of their lives. Ah, now we get to it. This is where my entrepreneur gene was born. My maternal grandparents were farmers for the entirety of their working lives and they brought up six children, of whom my mother was the youngest. The four eldest were all self-employed, and some of their children too, farmers and B&B owners in Dorset and award-winning cheese makers in Somerset.

But back to being the Odd One Out.

There was a bit of a ruckus when, aged 10, I refused to be confirmed into the Church of England, which is a bit weird frankly since I would now not have such issues although I do remain unconfirmed and 100% happy with that status. This didn't go well. It was my first painful rebellion and my father predicted that if I opted out of confirmation, I would be opting out for the rest of my life. Opting out, it can be inferred, was something of which he very strongly disapproved and in 1965 I must have screwed up every ounce of my courage as a little girl for this, my first personal stand. With hindsight, I would venture to say that opting-out was something of which he was fearful.

I don't know if that was his fear for me too or if he was being prescient but, as it turns out, never a truer word was said.

In my early days of rebellion and opting out, I revelled in it. I used to say that I had no idea I wanted to walk on the grass until you told me I could not. Ditto heavy petting in the shallow end if, Gentle Reader, you even know what that means; part of me hopes you will not. But rules and regs remain irksome, I'll confess. There's nothing I love more than a good entrepreneurial workaround, and I won't allow much to stand in my way if I am determined. This has not always turned out well, *nota bene*, especially where I have wilfully forced my own way on any particular set of circumstances, and often when computer has already said no. Once a client phoned me and said he'd been having a conversation with a third party, both of whom we knew, him more than me. The second chap was explaining to my client something I'd said, without naming me. The first chap said he just knew it was me, it had my classic hallmark of reverse engineering all over it, finding creative ways to achieve the desired outcome and working backwards from said outcome to find or discover or invent the route to success.

I no longer need to make such silly protests as I've become surer in myself, except where it really matters, and I do have a couple of those up my sleeve right now, social and political injustices, neither of which are silly though protesting is involved. But in my work these days no rebellion is required, I just put my foot down assertively.

But Odd One Out I was and, to some extent, Odd One Out I remain, though I will tell you this and proudly too - there are serious amounts of entrepreneurial thinking and radical alternative brainpower amongst my closest family members, the ones who are very much still alive and kicking and working in - yes, hush my mouth - jobs. Or jobs-ish. You definitely can, if you choose, be entrepreneurial in their sort of work. Indeed, I believe it is even encouraged in some quarters.

Most of my friends are not self-employed either, with one notable exception. My oldest school friend is Leslie Scott, the inventor of Jenga. At that time, I was her accountant and we learned much together about the perils and pitfalls of being entrepreneurs.

A close friend is an employee, a terrific one, she knows how to "go along to get along", something which simply is not in my DNA. Kudos to her, whereas they call me "razor sharp and blunt". I am not sure you can be both blunt and employed. Is that even possible? Can employees speak their minds? It certainly didn't work for me in those fateful four jobs I held for a few moments way back in the Seventies.

But all the rest of my friends, companions, colleagues and clients are drawn from the ranks of entrepreneurs, the self-employed, business owners, contractors, micro businesses, solopreneurs and freelancers, and I love the very bones of them, of you.

These are my people, my tribe, my posse. I know you through and through, inside and out, and you me. I have 40 years' experience of being you.

You are where I feel most at home, understood and appreciated and vice versa. This is where I can be most truly myself. You make me feel normal and, at times, that's precisely what I need to feel in amongst my peers, with other folk just like me. I know you know this feeling when those around you who love you serve only to help you to feel misunderstood, an outsider, a weirdo and just plain wrong and bonkers even though that may not always be their intention, or at all. I know it because you tell me so.

Deep down, I have no idea why I felt the strongest of strong urges to follow this path to entrepreneur heaven (and hell), there just didn't seem to be any alternative. With me, what you see is what you get, and that didn't ever seem to be desirable in a job. Maybe these anecdotes and ponderings will go some way towards explaining it because I usually like to try to understand and make sense of almost everything that is within the grasp of my intelligence, such as it is. But in the final analysis, it doesn't really matter.

Oddball I have been, but no more. I feel it less and less. I am letting that name just fall away, no need to take pride in it anymore because us oddballs and weirdos are becoming the new normal.

People are being called to be self-employed in greater numbers than ever before. Well, not ever before, but certainly since the Industrial Revolution and the rush to jobs in factories and offices. Jobs are not working for people and, in this century, jobs are not as plentiful either as they were when first I returned to London in 1977, after a brief spell of living in Oxford with undergraduate school friends.

In London way back then you could buy the Evening Standard on your day of arrival and have both a job and somewhere to live by teatime. I know! It beggars belief by comparison to modern times, doesn't it? But this is how it was, honest to God.

And so I did just that. I got a job at a firm of accountants in Dulwich Village and a flat in Peckham, both on the same day, and then a little later I bought my first home in Herne Hill with a £500 loan from my Dad, which he later said I need not repay. And that's where my adventures in self-employment began, along with getting my ears pierced, buying my first car and starting to build a life for myself, all in my 23rd year.

I remember the turning point very well. It was thinking through this logic: all the advice I'd received from my parents, though lovingly intended and wisely endowed, simply wasn't working for me. I had to go my own way, which was pretty much 180 degrees in the opposite direction. At Secretarial College they taught me that girls and sums don't mix. That's probably wrong too then, Judith? I began to question everything.

Employment generally hadn't gone well for me. I mostly thought I was brighter than all the men I worked for and I wanted them to pay me at least three times what they thought I was worth to do their typing and filing, dial their phone calls for them (Dear God in Heaven!), make their tea and wash up afterwards thankyouverymuch. And, now that I come to think about it, I don't remember many thanks; these were thankless tasks. After a brief stint in London and then three years in Oxford, four jobs in four years, I started freelancing with said firm of accountants and it felt like coming home. Sums were the first thing I remember loving that loved me back. If you are even nearly as old as me, you might know I "borrowed" that phrase from Rhoda Morgenstern who said it of food.

In 1982/3 I went out on my own, not initially through my own choice (I was eventually fired, can you imagine?) and started my own accountancy business. It was accidentally quite the right time to do it in Mrs Thatcher's entrepreneurial Britain. Where I lived in South London it seemed everyone was starting their own business and they all wanted someone to cook the books. Fifteen years later I had built it into something which had its own premises, a staff of six, and over 250 clients. It had a life of its own, independent of me. It was my first baby, by now a teenager, ready to go onwards without me.

By 1996 the fun had gone out of it for me, so I sold it in early 1997. I realised I wasn't a career accountant, though I did love sums and, on occasion, I still do. I realised that I am an entrepreneur and entrepreneurship is about creativity, about making something come alive into the world that wasn't here before. Like parents and procreation, my businesses have been my babies. My thing is business, but for lots of my clients today it is art and writing and all manner of creativity. If you can dream it, you can make a self-employed living out of it. You can employ yourself for money.

By 1997 I had created, sold and disposed of several businesses in accounting, travel, and catering. My Mum worked with me in one of the catering ones but she was really my employee, it felt safer for her that way, although we were, in fact, partners in the enterprise and she brought lots of herself to it and to its success, including her fondly remembered piccalilli. That's key. Bringing lots of yourself to it. Take note. The Daphne Morgan School of Entrepreneurship. In fact, she would have been a natural. She had ideas and just a dash of spiv too, handy at a boot fair. Love a bit of spiv, me.

I was exhausted by this point in my entrepreneurial story. My father had died and I realised that a lot of my efforts in business had been failed attempts to get him to notice me, and approve of me, and show me he was proud of my achievements. But he wasn't. This wasn't the way in which he measured success in a woman. He wanted me to be happily married and with a family and sadly he came to realise that was never my own goal, he'd shot himself in the foot and had over-educated me for that. I was opinionated and too clever by half, and simply incapable of compromise. Way back then it was my way or… well, my way.

I took five years off work between 1997 and 2002, though I still did some part-time accounting to keep my hand in for clients where I believed I made a unique personal contribution, and to give my working week some framework while I set out to discover how I wanted to express my various talents next. I travelled and studied almost everything you could name, from public speaking to wine-tasting, wanting to find out where business could and would take me. I was looking for something lighter and easier that I could be just as passionate about and, like my Mum, where I could bring myself to work even more elegantly than I had done as an accountant.

In 2002 I discovered coaching. I knew this new business had my name all over it because I had always intuitively coached my accounting clients, it came free with me doing their VAT return. I just didn't know that was what it was called. I helped and boosted and supported them into believing they could do it. And so they could. And so they did. It is nothing short of amazing what just a little bit of unconditional love will do. Being their accountant was my delivery vehicle for the coaching. I just dropped the bit I had come to find stressful and unrewarding in every way, but not before I'd learned some very valuable business lessons about which I teach my clients today and which have also shaped my own current endeavours.

Love is a big part of this for me. I loved my clients and my work, not to the exclusion of all else, but before all else. And as a single woman this accounts (geddit?) for a lot of my success at work because I have the space and the focus and the freedom to put my work first. No-one to pay my bills for me so I'd better make some money myself; frightened of failing though less so these days because entrepreneurial life knocks that out of you, and proud as punch of the businesses I have created, sold and franchised, and the management buy-outs I have facilitated, all in the name of helping others to be successfully self-employed.

Passion? Some days it feels more like a mission!

In 2002 when I started coaching, my advisers wanted me to specialise in looking after small business owners since they had always been my stock in trade. Then I was still screaming "No, no, no!" and running in the opposite direction. It took me a while to come back down to earth and realise they were right, this is where my cred lies, this is who and what I know through and through. 2017 marks the 40th anniversary of my self-employment, what on earth else would I want to do but help others with that?

Once I started down that track, what my new clients wanted me to do was teach them how to run a small business, how to work successfully for themselves. They wanted me to take everything I had learned the hard way and make it easy for them, and knock about seventeen years off it so that they could do it in three. Or less. They wanted business acumen and acceleration and make it snappy!

The truth is that business at this level is easy and you can learn it pretty quick, not overnight but yes, you ought really to be seeing some serious results within three years, for sure. Yep, I know, shock, horror! But it is true. There is very little to master, and what you can never master you simply outsource, accounting for starters.

But here's the truly fascinating bit. And the reason for writing this book, and writing it now in the summer of 2017.

Somewhere in the years between 2002 and 2017 my clients started to want something completely different from me. I think they know subliminally too that business at our level is easy and so what they do (and I still have no real idea why they do this, nor do I much care why) is to bring me all sorts of adjacent and overlapping issues of a personal development nature for me to help them unpick. They trust me with this personal stuff most close to their hearts, their innermost secrets, fears, anxieties, neuroses, procrastinations and problems which they allow to sabotage their success and forward movement in their self-employment and businesses. And where I am going to share those in this book, I either have their permission or I have sought to protect their anonymity. Those who are out and proud are named in the Roll of Honour at the back of the book and appreciated beyond measure for their bravery.

This work is wonderful for me and wondrous to me. If I were still teaching what clients wanted to learn in 2002 I'd be outta here by now. But because my clients have morphed in those fifteen years and manifested as much more interesting and complex people, they have provided me with the opportunity to become precisely what my friends and family feared when I set up shop as a coach - an amateur psychologist.

That was never my intention. But it is where I've ended up. Go figure. Life! Honestly, you couldn't make it up, and what with its never-ending twisty-turnyness there's never a dull day, thankfully. I never know what my clients will bring me next. How exciting is that? What infinite variety! Equally, I feel 100% sure that I will be able to help…try me. I've seen and helped to solve everything. As I often say, I am somewhat like a doctor in that I no longer notice your nakedness though I am mindful of it always.

I've been called to this work by you, my clients. You are my great teachers. Everything you tell me I believe even though I have never felt some or all of it first-hand but I absolutely believe it to be true, to be what you are experiencing in your own life and business. Forgive me for saying "in my day", I will try not to say it too often, but in my day we were not bedevilled by such matters. Personal development hadn't really been invented and we just had a go and it mostly seemed to work out alright. We were less complex human beans and we definitely lived in simpler times. We just cracked on. It was the wild wild west of self-employment and regulation was comparatively non-existent. We were younger and fearless and powerful, hungry for success. We just went for it. But you are not like that, I know. S'ok. Your secret's safe with me. It is somewhat of an open secret around these parts - shh!

Now, some things in my business career have very definitely not been easy. I was born in 1955 which means I have weathered TWO global recessions/financial meltdowns, and both times I have lost my shirt yet hung onto my businesses by the skin of my teeth. And now, at the time of writing, by dint of my date of birth again, my pension has been delayed by six years until I am 66 so I have no choice but to keep working. By the time

Her Majesty's Government deems it is time to pay me my pensioner's due and mite, I shall have been in gainful work and contributing to that pension for 48 years. Unbelievable, even and especially to me, not that I was ever in it for the pension but still.

How fortunate, then, that I love my work.

The world has a knack of sideswiping us. When I look back I have weathered those storms and they have, at times, been inordinately tough, tougher than I can possibly convey. I have done it mostly alone, hiding away through the worst times, though I have been supported in all crucial ways by family love and even bailed out by them too in terrible times and awful frightening circumstances of fear and loss. I'm not sure they understood so much as that they were prepared to support. There's some of that unconditional love again, not a feature of my childhood but very definitely one of my adult life, lucky girl that I am.

And here I am, still standing as Elton would say. They say that what doesn't kill you makes you stronger. I wish it wasn't so; I could stand it a whole lot easier and less life-threatening than that. I wish I hadn't been buffeted by those oh-so destructive forces. But I hope I have demonstrated that there's nothing you can tell me or show me which will surprise me, at least I know your worst fears and nightmares even if not first hand. There's nothing I haven't felt or don't believe when you tell it to me because a thousand of your predecessors have shared it with me also.

If it is true for you, then it's true. End of. I get you. I'll hold you while you learn this too. You are safe, protected and loved. It is safe for you to be self-employed, to ask other people for money and to run your own small business. It's not going to kill you, even if it goes bust. Running out of money doesn't lead to instant death or even a slow lingering one. And most of what we fear never comes to pass.

I don't judge. My aim always is to help you to find a way to bust through the bonkersness you are putting in your own way so that you can employ yourself for money.

What I want for you is Your Biz Your Way. I want you to learn to trust yourself and to be able to relax because you've got this. Chill! This is all going to go much better if you will just exhale. Breathing is something we do a lot in my coaching and mentoring sessions when the emotions threaten to engulf us, or when you are talking so fast that even I (fast thinker, fast talker) cannot keep up. Breathe. We need some space, some time. Breathe, you've got this.

You can be as weird-ass as you like and still make money in your microbusiness, working from home at the kitchen table or garden shed or simply from your smartphone. You can have a freelance life of freedom which you will totally love. It will work around your kids. It'll be better than a J.O.B. You're gonna love it, just as soon as you ditch all the bonkersness. Take it from me. It's not going to happen overnight, so dig in. Dig in for victory. And hold on for the ride of your life.

My hope with this book is that, in sharing the bonkersness 2017-stylee that my clients bring to me, you will be able to see that you are just like them and me and that we are all entirely normal. And that we can all do this self-employment thing. It isn't hard except that we make it so.

And so I will end on one of my very favourite coaching expressions of all time, all my own work this one, and which I will add I only use in extremis: **Stop it immediately**. Stop with the bonkersness. Lay it down. You've made it up, you've hallucinated it as my favouritest-ever coach, Michael Neill, would say.

What follows in this book are some typical examples of everyday entrepreneurial bonkersness in 2017, and you will recognise yourself on almost every page whether or not it actually IS you. These questions and conundrums come from my real self-employed clients and colleagues who are all human beings just like me and you, they are not exceptional in any way because anyone can do this, just like anyone can drive a car. There's not even a test for this though one of my book-keepers, the immortal and unforgettable Coral, used to think that there should be and some days I can see where she was coming from!

We are all in this together. We are all the Odd One Out and you are not nearly as odd as me, frankly. If you want to win that contest, you are going to have to up your game considerably. We are all unique, and working for yourself is the greatest privilege and adventure ever.

Now, with all that preamble out of the way, let's crack on.

Judith Morgan
London, England
August 2017

YOUR BIZ
YOUR WAY

CHAPTER ONE

Bonkersness

Question 1

HAVE I LEFT IT TOO LATE?

I checked with you before I answered this one. I wanted to know how old you are. And you told me that you are "45 - just starting a second career as an entrepreneur after 20 years in communications and marketing. Got to the top of the ladder and didn't like the view!"

45. Dear God, you are a CHILD!

OK, we can do this scientifically, or we can do it based on our beliefs. Or both.

You are going to outlive your mother and her mother. By a long chalk. I am planning to live until I am 100 and you are going to probably outlive that because you are 20 years younger than me. The outliving your mother and her mother thing comes about because you are a woman and what happened to their lives and health and death has some genetic impact, to the extent you choose to believe it does, on yours. Both my parents shortened their own lives (booze and fags), but my grandparents lived until their mid-80s and that was two generations ago. So I'm on for 100. At least.

So you have 55 years left in you, possibly more. Imagine! I'll wait while you do that…

I once went to a workshop with Michael Neill and he got us to do this exercise where you draw a grid on a piece of paper which is 6 squares by 5, representing the next thirty years of your life. And you write into each box your plans for as far into the future as you can possibly imagine. When I did that exercise, I only used up the first three boxes with all my wild and extravagant plans for the rest of my life, which left me 27 years free at the end of that. Which was precisely what Michael wanted us to see. See further tips on how to do this exercise below.

There is plenty of time. For everything.

There is no shortage of time, that's an illusion. You know all those things you read about how short life is? Stuff and nonsense! Life isn't short for most of us although I'll grant you it can sometimes feel like that.

You know how when you are doing something you love, time goes really quickly? And when you are doing something you hate or dread, or when you are wishing your life away, the hands on the clock slow down or even stop. Time drags. I used to go to Italian classes at the tech in the evenings when I was at boarding school. Even though that was my choice and I loved learning Italian, I would watch and listen to the clock and every single one of those 120 minutes tick by and feel every single one of those 7,200 seconds. Waiting for the lift, or the bus, or anything you are impatient about, feels interminable, doesn't it?

There is loads of time, honestly. Nothing is ever too late.

I take lots of comfort from all those stories you read about people who started things "later" in life. 45 isn't late, it's barely past early. It will flash in the blink of an eye, yes. And it does appear to go faster the older you get. But there's still loads of it, and it's stretchy.

I just thought I'd Google for you - achievers in later life - and straight away I found a wonderful article on Psychology Today called The Top Ten Late Bloomers of All Time (which neither of us is, by the way, you starting again at 45 least of all) and it is subtitled "never too late for old dogs to do new tricks"!

EXACTLY! I rest my case.

I know you know this is bonkers. Time to stop believing in the messages from that other side of you, the side that isn't really you at all.

Try Michael's exercise. Get a piece of paper, draw a box on it, a grid which is six squares by five giving you thirty in all. Make the boxes as big as you need. At the top write either the years - 2017, 2018, 2019 etc. Or how old you are - 62, 63, 64. Now write into the boxes all your plans and hopes and dreams for as far into the future as you have worked that out already, time-wise. What do you discover?

And enjoy this article from The Guardian newspaper:
https://www.theguardian.com/lifeandstyle/2017/aug/28/meet-women-launching-startups-50s-deep-breath-jumped

Question 2

WHY DO I FEEL I MUST DO IT ALL MYSELF?

"Why can't I accept help from my husband?"

A lot of my female (and male) clients share this particular brand of bonkersness and, in some households, you can't accept help from your other half because it simply isn't available or they are unable or unsympathetic, or both.

Equally, many of us feel the pull to be independent, even within a marriage or a partnership. We want to earn money and pay our way.

And how interesting this question comes from a woman who I know to be a giver. Interesting, but perhaps not a surprise.

The world tends to fall into two camps, the givers and the takers. Not exclusively, but ish.

And we givers are not very good at taking, or asking for support which might be freely given were we to make our need known. 'Cos sometimes you have to do that, make your need known and ask, especially if it all looks great from the outside or you have a history of self-reliance.

Balance, of course, is being equally able to give and receive in any relationship or environment. It's all a bit broken if it's loppy (lop-sided).

There's a very real joy in achieving something all by yourself. I know this very well. And we feel proud and happy when we do. But nothing is taken away from us when we do things in partnership either. *Au contraire*. It may provide your husband with a wonderful means by which he can show his love and support if he's one of those who cannot use words to demonstrate that. Or even if he can, he may want to do this as well.

Lots of my clients have supportive other halves. And a few have the other sort, and I know which one I'd prefer. But even when they do have supportive types, they wish they didn't need to lean on them. They crave independence.

A couple of thoughts, then… with the intention of being useful always:

1. A supportive partner is a safety net. And sometimes that means you either don't take risks or are less likely to, or you don't want to if you feel you are playing fast and loose with his support as opposed to just with your own resources. Or maybe you feel you must take into account his advice with his support and that would cramp your artistic style in some way, or involve a compromise you are unwilling to make?

2. But that safety net could also be a fantastic asset. It could enable you to fly without looking down. It could enable you to do all sorts of aerial acrobatics, walk between two tall buildings on a tightrope, do stunts. With his support, you could scale greater heights. You could be greater than the sum of your parts. You could love and be loved. This is a two-way

street, remember? It is what you both promised you'd do for each other. For all I know you've already supported him in ways that have enabled his success, and from which he can now return the favour. You probably downplay them, or have forgotten, or didn't even notice you were doing that because it is just your nature. And what if him supporting you was just his?

Take it from a woman who's done it all (or mostly) by herself all her life, it isn't better. Or worse. It's just different. And harder. Much, much harder.

In fact, recently I realised when playing and teaching Rich Dad's Cashflow 101 game, which is something I've done hundreds of times, that it simply isn't possible to make it work in the mathematics of our modern world by yourself. The two of you are a team and together you succeed, not separately.

A dear old friend fondly remembered, a man, once saw me struggling to open a bottle of wine by myself. We shared a great friendship, and he offered to help me by doing it for me. I said "No, it's OK, I can do it" and he said "I **know** you can do it. Let me help". He was looking for a space in my life, for me to be less independent, he wanted to demonstrate his care for me by doing something I could do quite capably myself but he could do better and more easily and, above all, lovingly. He wanted to help. He wanted to support. Yin and Yang, remember, Judith? Make room for the poor chap. Nudge over a tad. Make room for help.

As with everything, seek the balance. Sometimes we go it alone. Sometimes we are grateful for support. Sometimes we do it as a team.

Have you had a discussion with your husband about this? I'd love to hear it from his perspective. Does he need or want you to do it all by yourself? How would he feel if you did?

Are you putting unrealistic expectations upon yourself? Why?

Start to examine your own bonkersness and, in time, all this stuff falls away.

What could it mean if you accepted help? Write down all the answers which occur to you, until your truth reveals itself.

Do you know how to do tapping (EFT)? If so, tap away the negative ones which might be disabling you. If not, pop into the Ask Judith Facebook Group and ask and I'll point you in the right direction.

Question 3

WHY AM I ALWAYS COMPELLED TO START A NEW NOTEBOOK?

"The 'I'll start a new notebook for that idea' syndrome means I always have many, many, notebooks on the go at any one time, plus bookmarks in Pocket and in different browsers, helpful ideas and notes on my phone, books laid open where I was taking notes… the resulting visual chaos means that from time to time I simply tidy everything away and start again."

What happens when you tidy everything away? Do you lose your notes and ideas? Are they replaced by others?

I've written elsewhere in this book about Ideas Sex, how seductive a gazillion ideas are and how much we creative types adore them. But they don't pay the bills, do they?

I too love a bit of stationery and suffer from stationery lust. Only this week my client showed me her new notebook, so I bought one even though I don't need one! I've since paid it forward to my niece who has the stationery thing and accepted it gratefully, sight unseen.

There are a couple of useful thoughts which come to mind. It's an either/or I think.

Either

Carry on as you are. Collect all your thoughts and ideas and write them down for fear of losing them.

OR

Trust that the Universe has got your back and that you will remember anything important, or your subconscious will. I think there's a scarcity (and a lack of trust in our memory too) that we scrabble to write everything down. Ironically, as you probably know, smart woman that you are, our memory works better the more we use and trust it to work as it should, as it does just naturally if we will but allow it.

I don't have notes all over the shop. I use one notebook at a time but you are beginning to get to know me by now. Discipline is one of my middle names! I'll confess I do keep the odd note or list on that thingie on my iPad, but I think they currently number four and I've owned this iPad since 2011. So you get my drift.

Next time you feel the need to bookmark something or start a new notebook, don't. See what happens instead. See what it feels like. See if you lose something valuable forever. Or see if you just feel easier and you sigh in relief. I'm betting you will.

In a nutshell, hoarding ideas is scarce. They are in unlimited abundance and available to us to download from divine escrow whenever we want. Action is the thing. Am I going to action this today or soon? If no, then how will it help me if I record it for posterity?

There's no shortage of ideas, nor ever will be. We could trust that our memory and our sub-conscious and our genius always has full access to all of the ideas we've ever created or, at the very least, the important ones or the ones we are determined we are going to do something with. If we aren't going to do something with them, and we don't want to hug notebooks full of them to ourselves (not quite sure what the point of that would be?), then we don't need to record them. I have a sense that recording them is just contributing to your overwhelm which is why, eventually, you let them free, releasing them back into the wild or the WPB, whichever is handier on the day.

What I *do* do is review each notebook as it becomes full. Sometimes as I move from the old to the new, I keep the just-past-finished one for a bit, then one day I go through it and bring forward to the newer notebook anything important. And occasionally, if that becomes repetitive, or in the case of something I want people to access after my death (!), I record it somewhere on my computer, although God alone knows how they will break into that.

This is a major bonkersness on both our parts, isn't it?

Ideas are not gold-dust. They are in a never-ending and plentiful supply, that's part of the problem. Accept them, appreciate them, love them, let them come and go knowing they are all around us all the time, even when we are sleeping. And stop with the need to record them.

Just to play devil's avocado* in closing, many creative people *comme nous* die with homes full of notebooks crammed with snippets, creativity prompts, cuttings and ideas. If that's you, then keep on keeping on. Only you can decide if this habit is doing more harm than good, for that's all I believe it is, a habit. And you can decide whether that's a good and supportive habit, or not. By the sound of it, the answer is not. And, if so, you already know what I am going to say, don't you? **Stop it immediately!**

* Thanks to J and C for this gorgeous expression. You know who you are.

NOTES

- **What else are you collecting and hoarding?**
- **What else could you release?**
- **I wonder what creative gorgeousness might drop into that void?**

Question 4

WHY AM I PLAGUED BY APPARENTLY INSURMOUNTABLE OBSTACLES?

"There appears to be a part of my personality that, having noticed a good plan and way forwards is evolving, slowly unravels the idea by placing apparently insurmountable technical, practical and/or financial obstacles in my line of sight until I lose interest in it."

Yep, I hear ya. Been there, done that, got the T-shirt.

It is a form of self-sabotage I believe. Those come in all shapes and sizes, don't they, the little blighters?

I vaguely remember that I won a consultation with a guru at some point in the last fifteen years or so. I cannot remember who or what he was and I had no idea what I was going to talk to him about. I have another vague memory of meeting him in a restaurant somewhere in London, but again that might not be what happened.

I do remember what he told me though.

I said to him that I was getting very, very close to getting what I wanted out of life at that time. The things that had been on my vision board for a few years were looming and about to manifest (I'd been putting my back into it, my go-to system in those days). And, the closer they got, the more I changed my mind about what I wanted. I explained that I'd been in that game so long, the things I thought I wanted appeared to be changing, as was I.

And he said carry on to the end anyway. Complete. Finish the work and the manifestation. Because in that way we train ourselves and carve out new neural pathways that we are successful people, that we are completer-finishers, that we can have whatever we want and we then can point to experiences of having done that so we know it's true about ourselves.

I know this was very wise advice. He was saying stop changing your mind all the time. Keep your eyes on the prize, get the prize, and re-focus on a new one. Rinse and repeat. In so doing we reinvent ourselves as achievers who can have whatever we want whenever we want it and our catalogue of successful results and achievements grows, which helps us to feel powerful and to know about ourselves that anything is possible for us.

I notice in your use of the word "apparently" that this isn't the truth. It's just a get-out if you want it. This is a get-out I have used often, especially if a mountain needs to be climbed. I have noticed it even as I've written this book, procrastinating every day, thinking no-one would notice if I welshed on my word. That's not true, and I would notice most of all.

Here's a useful resource which I think you will LOVE. It's a website called Because I Said I Would and the idea is to help and support all of us to become true to our word and carry through on something we have promised ourselves or others that we would do. As with everything, I think this is easier to do for others than it is for myself often, but I think it is equally important, if not more so, to do it for myself. Being a woman of my word is one of my top values. And you can see how it would help you too to bust through the apparent obstacles.

I suppose what we are talking about here is being or becoming determined, determined enough to bust through those obstacles which are no more than mere illusions. Oh, what a tricksy so-and-so our ego is, all in the name of protecting us from failure and disappointment. So much easier to manifest a whole long queue of obstacles which makes it "impossible" for us to have what we said we wanted.

Changing your mind is one thing, generally a good thing as I write later in the book, especially if you are wrong. I've done that and will do that again and again. I suppose where the woman of your word comes in is in not committing to anything you know you won't actually do and push through to the end on. I know you are a woman of ideas. Time to start grading them and only working on the ones you feel like Superwoman about so that you know you can complete on them, whatever appears over the horizon.

Again, I have a sense that this is a habit which, once outed and busted, will just wither and die, imposter that it is.

Because I Said I Would also supply some gorgeous little cards on which you can write promises to yourself and to others, and pledges. And you can swap them with your friends and family, and with me.

- I will not allow any obstacle to get in my way.
- I will complete this project.
- I will do everything in my power to keep my interest alive.

https://becauseisaidiwould.com/

Question 5

WHAT MAKES THE FOLLY OF MULTIPLE PROJECTS SO SEDUCTIVE?

"The 'there's safety in numbers' multiple-projects-on-the-go-at-any-one-time theory, despite all evidence to the contrary."

I love this. I love it especially because you tell me your own answer. "Despite all evidence to the contrary." Quite.

And you already know that playing with multiple projects simultaneously is precisely the way to prove yourself right, that it is a folly.

I think it leaks. What I mean by that is if you don't believe in your own project enough to make it your one and only (or your one and only for now) that vibe leaks and your ideal client/customer picks up on that somehow.

I think you have to be on fire with your #1 offering and give it all you've got and that vibe is precisely what it takes to make it, or anything, work.

The confusion can sometimes come in knowing which one to pick.

I know you a little, and that's enough for me to know that deep down you also know which is The One. With my clients, it is often the one they save till last on our induction call. The one where they go "Of course, what I've always REALLY wanted to do is…" It's The One they hold closest to their chest because they fear showing it to the light in case it withers to dust after all these years, or I don't like it or others don't like it or it doesn't work or any manner of one or more examples of bonkersness.

As your coach, there are lots of ways I could get you to choose just one.

There's that hoary old chestnut where I pretend to hold a gun to your head or kidnap your first born or something. On pain of death, which one would you choose then?

I've fiddled about with multiple businesses and multiple projects and I was just limiting my own success. So perhaps the more pertinent question is why on earth would you do that?

Two final thoughts (a quick question this):

1. See my piece Q33 about Ideas Sex. That's all the multiple projects are. Safety perhaps. Seduction certainly.

2. See my blog article called One Woman One Website. One project properly done, to the exclusion of all else, is enough for one woman and what it takes to be successful as a solopreneur. It is a full-time job just making one work successfully to the point where it will bring you the results you seek, whatever they may be. One Thing = One Winner. You can do the other ones once your needs are taken care of. Once you have trained your brain to do one thing at a time, Sweet Jesus.

https://www.judithmorgan.com/one-woman-one-website/

Question 6

HOW DO I DECIDE WHAT'S "REAL" WORK?

"Procrastination tasks that almost look like real work - the "I'll just create some art for that calendar" detour instead of the harder, more linear tasks that would move me further forward."

When I wrote to my Small Business Big Magic group about why weren't they blogging more, my Feedly feed being void of their creative output and me missing it, K replied:

"I do a bit, but I seem to go through bursts. Right now it's a "write articles and blog to avoid real work" phase that I need to break free from."

K's distinction is very interesting to me. He sees writing articles and blogging as a way to avoid real work. I see both of those as real work. And I note your distinction too, although yours look very much more like "proper" procrastination detours. And you are right.

In my "real work" as K would call it, I do not procrastinate mainly due to long decades of experience, high levels of discipline, self-discipline and habit, all of which can be trained into you by the way. Also high levels of motivation and inspiration, neither of which need training. Currently I can't wait to get up and get at it, however much I LOVE a lie in. And oh boy, do I love a lie in. Even on Saturdays and Sundays, I want to get up and get to my work when I am on fire with it, as I have been writing this book.

But when I started to write, I found new levels (depths?) of previously undiscovered, and unexplored procrastination I didn't even know existed down there, and I certainly didn't know I had the capacity to enjoy them so much!

I've discovered it is very much a part of my creative writing habit, to fanny and faff about for a bit first. In the end, I bore myself and I turn to. I think also this procrastination opportunity is very much facilitated by it being August which alongside it already having a lovely laid back quasi-holiday vibe means I also have time to procrastinate over my writing 'cos that's pretty much all I have scheduled myself to do this month. I am off from the podcast and off from my 1-2-1 clients. If I were as busy as normal months, I wouldn't have the luxury of this. And it does feel quite luxurious.

But I notice that I am running out of time. Everything's relative of course, but I gave myself August to write the book or at least get the words out, and it's 21st already and I have more than ten days' work left and I had planned to take off the entirety of the final week. I suspect my procrastination will have cost me that.

That's a good point, isn't it? What is your procrastination costing you? You have sent me a few questions about avoidance which prompts me to think of what a proper coach would ask you - what's the anti-goal? How do you win by doing the tasks that almost look like real work?

Work that out, then bust it. Trick yourself into doing it the other way. You could go for simple bribery as I often do - no coffee until X, no watching Mike and Harvey in Suits until Y etc. Ha! Had to do that earlier this month when doing someone's accounts as I am sure you read me say on Facebook. In my normal work where I do marketing so that I can be with clients, in neither of those do I procrastinate. Just in this area of being an author.

Now, where's that article about Procrastination being a good and creative thing? Oh yes, here it is. I hesitate to give you even more permission to go round the houses but I wonder what it would be like to think of it positively rather than negatively? Try it on for size and let me know.

"According to research". It must be true then! LOL.

https://tinyurl.com/MediumProcrastinating

BREATHING SPACE – CHAPTER ONE - BONKERSNESS

This is a luxurious space for you and your thoughts at the end of each chapter, each bunch of questions. What, if anything, spoke to your own bonkersness in this first chapter? Questions 1-6 are about age, doing it all yourself, new notebook compulsive disorder (NNCD), apparently insurmountable obstacles, multiple project folly and learning how to discern between real work and procrastination.

Was there anything in there that rang a bell or pushed your buttons?

What did you learn about yourself and your business, or were you reminded about?

Where do you agree with me, or disagree? How does that help you to trust yourself more and more in creating your own biz your way?

How will you change as a result of what you've read, or is it simply a matter of deciding to be just a little bit more confident from this day on?

Here's a lovely space for you to take some time out, breathe, think through what you've read and write some notes for yourself based on your own thoughts arising. If there's anything in here you want to ask me about or share, do pop into the Ask Judith Facebook Group. That applies to anything you discover in the Breathing Spaces at the end of each chapter in this book.

JUDITH MORGAN

CHAPTER TWO

Feelings

Question 7

I'M UNSURE. WHAT CAN I DO AND FOR WHOM?

In my experience, this problem arises from the over application of the logical brain. When I was grappling with this myself, it turned out it was right under my nose, the place where the answer to this question often resides. Of course, that choice of home for this little lovebucket makes it particularly invisible, especially to us, and blindingly obvious to others.

Three questions might help.

1. What's your cred? What's in your life and in your career to date and in your CV that will impress potential future clients and enable them to resonate with your story and think "Yes! This is the woman for me. This is the woman who understands what it is to be me, and who has the cred to help me sort myself out." It is in plain sight. So write down a whole long list of the things you've done, the places you've been, the people you've met, your achievements, the things people always say to you, the plaudits you've received, a long long list adding up to what the world already appreciates you for. It doesn't mean you are going to work in any of those areas, these accomplishments are simply a box for you to stand

on and from which to appreciate the full glory of who you are. I know, I know. You'll probably be a bit modest and uncomfortable with that unless you are quite Starry*. But you could always do this exercise with a friend or a series of people who have known you forever and appreciated you in lots of different ways - for your qualities, the things they've seen you be and do they've always been slightly envious of, the reasons they'd want you in their corner. Try to set modesty aside and come up with the best possible CV you can. Not a real CV, you understand. We are not going for a job here. It's more of an audit of your life to date, to go all accountant-y on you there for a mo.

2. The same next, but this time for your private enthusiasms and passions. What are you going to love to help people with every day for the rest of your life? Ish. I won't hold you to it and, over the years, this can morph and change. What can't you help yourself doing? For instance, today is the first day of my holiday and it is a Saturday. It is only 7.42 in the morning but I decided the thing I couldn't help but do today was to write my book, so I leapt out of bed, got an enormous coffee and I'm already 400 words into it! That. Imagine that you are on holiday, just like me. You have a list of relaxing and fun things you are going to do, you want to do, but your sub-conscious knows better. Mine wants to write this morning, in lieu of a lie-in which was on my list. What do you always come back to? What did you want to be as a teenager but it seemed so silly you set it aside? What have you always pursued even during the years you were in a job, even if only during your leisure time? What can you not imagine life without? All those sorts of exploratory questions, a lovely bit of navel gazing. Take yourself off somewhere uplifting with a gorgeous notebook, get creative fuels of choice and write it all down or draw it or record it somehow. The essential you. Give some thought to that thing that clients always say to me in the end. "Of course, what I've ALWAYS wanted to do is…" Some clients (very few) say to me (I honestly think they are pretending) that they don't know

what this is. It is because you have buried it so deeply because you never ever thought you'd be lucky enough to get the chance to do it, or because someone belittled you for it, or because it's very precious so you've put it away somewhere safe. You've almost forgotten about it. You can tell me. You can write it in that notebook, perhaps even with your "other" hand. I am SO not an artist but sometimes when we write with our other hand or we draw we are incredibly articulate and our subconscious speaks to us through our stick men. Whatever it takes, excavate that, reveal that.

3. Next, we are looking for the sweet spot where these two cross over. You have the credibility that people will buy it from you, and you have the passion to do it if not for the rest of your life, then for the foreseeable future while we build a business out of it.

Don't worry too much for now about the "for whom". Your ideal client will not be able to help themselves but gallop over your horizon once you have clarity about the what. Once you are on fire with the what, sufficient to love the idea of sharing it with the whole world, magnetising ICs to you and your lovely little biz is going to be a breeze.

Oh, and by the way, most of us start out without clarity. Be prepared to do that and these mists clear as you go. You are multi-talented. That's very much part of this because you could turn your hand to anything. You are infinitely able.

There are heroines of mine I can point you to, and I bet you can cite yours to me too, women and men who demonstrate that they started out as one thing and then morphed into another. My burning desire was to help people with their money and their small businesses. Firstly I did that as an accountant and now I do it as a coach and mentor and even as a writer, the thing I wanted to be as a teenager but parked it as no-one knew or encouraged it, not even me. The core desire is the same. To be of service in a particular metier. The way I do it constantly changes and that's what keeps my interest and passion alive.

NOTES

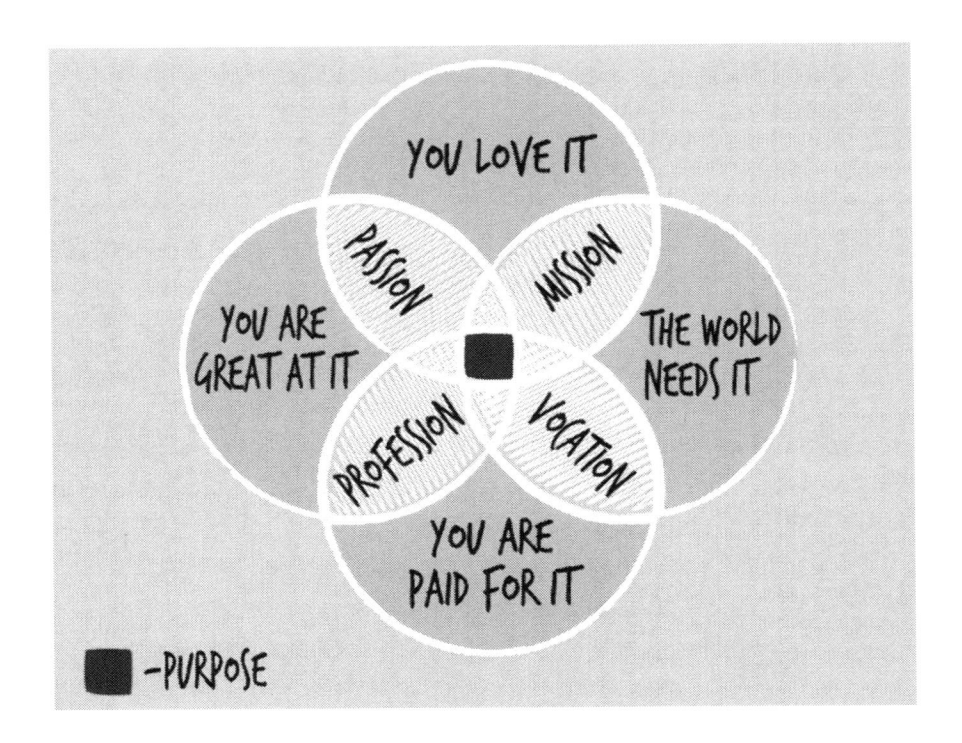

Ikigai diagram showing four overlapping circles: "YOU LOVE IT" (Passion/Mission), "THE WORLD NEEDS IT" (Mission/Vocation), "YOU ARE PAID FOR IT" (Vocation/Profession), "YOU ARE GREAT AT IT" (Profession/Passion), with the centre labelled as Purpose.

Question 8

HOW DO I SAY NO WITHOUT OFFENDING?

On the day I started writing this book, one of my dearest and oldest friends wrote to me. I am lucky to call her my friend and she is a very wise woman.

This summer we'd had occasion to support each other through making a difficult decision. She went one way, I went the other. To my eyes, this makes her the better person.

We'd both been invited to do something that neither of us particularly wanted to do. I'd consulted my friend about what she intended to do. She intended to do The Right Thing. I'd done what I wanted to do and taken the consequences, namely perhaps disappointing a couple of other people I care very much about in order not to upset myself. Tough choice. Rock and a hard place. I put myself first which is what I feel able to do when it comes right down to the wire and the choice is me or you. And I can only do it in my own favour when there are just those two stark choices. I have to choose me, all other things being vaguely equal. I can cite exceptions that prove the rule.

My friend wrote after the event "The older I get, the less inclined I am to do things I don't want to do" and I replied as follows.

"Being able to ask for our own needs to be met, and being OK about putting ourselves and those needs first, is something I teach my clients every day and something I have been learning to be OK with since I was 37 and, if you remember, on this occasion I still asked for your advice before I made my mind up!

In my work, we often call it "nice girl hand-wringing". It's where something makes us feel uncomfortable and we wring our hands but we do it anyway because we've been brought up to be a Nice Girl (or Boy). Decades of social and familial conditioning. But doing that, being a Nice Girl, makes us feel bad, often worse than bad; it is painful, it is like self-harming. So we do it at our own sometimes considerable cost.

One of the things I wrote in a tribute letter to my brother on the occasion of his recent 60th birthday was about this. It is something I learned from him and just one of a whole long list of things I love and appreciate about him.

You say things like "Do what you've got to do, Jude" even when it would suit you slightly (or even a lot) better if I did something else entirely.

On this occasion, I did what I had to do even though it might have suited *others if I had done something else entirely. I wish I could say I am without bad feelings about it. I am not. I should have done "the right thing". But I didn't want to, so I didn't. No doubt some would call that selfish, I accept that. It's part of my cost. It's even fair to a certain extent.*

Today I am starting to write my book and shall start with this very topic: Nice Girl Hand-Wringing."

Do you recognise yourself in this behaviour? Are you a Nice Girl or Boy who always does what's expected of you? Does it hurt? Well, **stop it immediately!** I know you aren't going to be able to stop people-pleasing behaviour overnight, I know you've been doing it as long as me and my friend.

I know you want to stop and I know it gets between you and running the sort of business you want. I know your friends and family and clients are putting upon you for all sorts of things you don't want to do and yet you are doing them anyway.

And you don't know how to get out of doing them, because you've always done them, and some of them are expected of you. And a few may remain so, especially if you are a parent to your own children and the dutiful daughter of parents still alive.

Warning! Once you start to say no, people won't like it. But they WILL get used to it. You will empower them to start doing these things for themselves instead, if they need doing at all. You'll be amazed by how the world shifts around you once you stop being so accommodating and put upon.

Those that don't like it will drift off and find some other sucker to fill their needs. Trust me, they will. I call those people "successful". It's a weird definition by which I mean they are successful at getting their needs met, mostly at the expense of others. You will read me reiterating this point in this book because I really believe it is worth underlining.

Let's give them, the drifter-offers, the benefit of the doubt and say they are unaware they are doing it. Yeah, right. At some level they know, but still… I'm giving them the benefit of the doubt. I'm a Nice Girl, remember?

When I'd done enough therapy and raised myself up to my full height and started to say no, this is how I saw it.

I was the driver of a Volvo estate car (bear with, this is a metaphor, I've never driven a Volvo estate except once, in Richmond Park, in the early Seventies and it didn't go well!) and it had one of those tow bars on the back and, behind me, weighing me down and slowing me down big time too was a very large and heavy caravan stuffed with a large number of passengers, standing room only and hanging out of every window and off the roof, a bit like an Indian train.

One day, I simply unhooked the caravan, all those carriages on the train. The people who really cared about me got into the Volvo and came with me, taking their turn at driving and giving to me and doing useful stuff for all of us on the team, like bringing the road trip mix tape, sharing snacks and map-reading.

I simply waved at those in the caravan as we accelerated away and they stayed where they were for a while, considering their options, before they simply got out and found another cosy home where someone else took care of them and their freaky needs.

Passengers. Relying on you. In a burdensome way. Let them go and free yourself.

Can you sense the relief already? I know you can. Go on, I dare you, unhook the caravan, say no, stop wringing your hands. You can do this. Don't save up all the hurt until you explode, just start to get your own needs met first whenever that's reasonable (most of the time). Not at all cost by any means, but first equal with everyone else's.

Do write and let me know how it goes!

NOTES

Who will you release and why?

How will life be better?

Question 9

WHY IS IT SO HARD TO HEAR MY OWN VOICE?

"I really liked your FB post about listening to your intuition vs. listening to what everyone else has to say. I know that the only way this will work is if I listen to myself but sometimes it's hard to distinguish who is saying what."

Gosh! I LOVE this one. How delicious is this?

I do hope that your question resonates with readers. I have a suspicion that it will.

This is the problem with all that received wisdom. Can I suggest you stop reading and listening and studying and imbuing everyone else with the wisdom and thinking it is outside of you, and start getting to know yourself better? The goal here is to trust yourself more. I already trust you, I think you have simply either never acquired the habit of trusting yourself or fallen out of the habit perhaps because of what life has thrown at you. I'd bet on that last one. We need to rebuild this muscle, that's all.

In that post, you saw me observe how long it took me and how much I was swayed by others when I was green. I say much the same thing in the introduction to this book too. It takes a while. But come the moment when you realise that everyone else's advice isn't working, it just gets easier to trust yourself from thereon in. There are many people I trust. But it doesn't mean I slavishly follow their advice or their way of doing things.

Let me illustrate by telling you about two of my friends.

The first one always asks my advice but never implements it. Once I realised that I was just one stop on her very long list of people she would consult simply by way of research, I stopped complying and started to say "What do *you* think?" I thought that she had so many other people she could ask that this was just a waste of my time.

The second friend does exactly the same thing, but in a way which is completely different and in a way which makes me happy. She asks me what I think when she's trying to make up her own mind about something. At first, I noticed how often she simply went off and did something completely different anyway and I was a bit sad about that until I realised it is part of her own magical way of being. My advice helps her make up her own mind, and that's very much how I like to be of service to my clients too.

Listen to what others think if you must (I don't bother with that much!), then make up your own mind. If you don't like your own decision, you'll soon know and can take a different path at the first crossroads, but both those paths will be your own choice and of your own taking.

I wonder what would help you with this? Imagine me in a thoughtful pose as I think about this!

Do you, for instance, journal every day? That's one way. Some of my clients favour a walk, especially if you do it in the spirit of knowing and trusting that your own answers will bubble up. It's the kinesiology, apparently. The opposite swinging of your arms with your walking legs. I know I haven't explained that very well, but if you swing your arms a bit more deliberately, your creative walk will be even more therapeutic.

I see both men and women have different ways of getting themselves into a trance, employing the busy part of their minds with cooking, driving, physical exercise, showering, anything that allows space for your own inner wisdom to come through.

The more you create a space for that wisdom to come through, the louder it will speak to you, always assuming you are quiet enough to hear. Get quiet. Pay attention.

The Facebook post to which my correspondent refers, written and published on 20th August 2017

"When I was 22 I became self-employed under the auspices of freelancing for a firm of accountants. This led quite quickly to my going out on my own and starting up what would become my own small business, my first one, in that same field of providing accounting to the people I still love to work with - small businesses and one woman/man bands.

However, all did not run smoothly. I fell in with a bad lot, a man my father called The Work-Shy Rogue, who persuaded me (it was VERY easy, I was still very young and quite green) that I would never make any money at my own business which required rather a lot of work and exchanging time for money and that we should, instead, go into property investing and various other money-making schemes.

Had I stuck to my guns, had I had enough self-belief, I would not have been susceptible to his blandishments or his schemes, the profits of which he drank and smoked away anyway. He didn't work. I did the work and funded it all and he lived off it. In the end, we lost everything and I was left hundreds of thousands of pounds in debt in 1992 and had to enter into an IVA, a voluntary arrangement with my creditors.

Had I just focused on my business, by the time I came to sell it in 1997, instead I would have been on a new BMW every three years and two Caribbean holidays each year (I got quite close to that anyway, not such a new car or as many holidays but my business provided funds for both). I would have E-Mythed it and I would still own it and it would be making money for me without my having to go into the office. Hindsight, eh? Mais je ne regrette rien.

The same thing happened when I went into coaching. I attracted huge amounts of received wisdom and advice that coaching is no way to make money. What a coach should do instead is learn to package herself up into books and coaching programmes and digital products, and that you'll never make any money just doing what you trained to do, namely be with your clients.

This time I HAVE resisted it. OK, I have managed to create a few investments around me which means I can perhaps more easily afford to be a largely 1-2-1 coach than some, but this isn't a business that can be easily E-Mythed, nor do I want it to be. And coaching isn't the easiest way to making a living in the world either, but it is possible and I know this because I have done it, I still do it every day.

The point of this story is that I realised as I was lying in bed this morning and thinking these thoughts that it is precisely the topic of my book - learning to trust yourself and not be swayed by others, learning to run Your Biz Your Way. What I teach is what I do."

This article makes reference to being E-Mythed. This expression is taken from a book by Michael Gerber called The E-Myth Revisited: Why Most Small Businesses Don't Work and What To Do About It. You will learn more about the value of The E-Myth later in this book.

Question 10

LOOK HOW GREAT *THEY* ARE. WHY ON EARTH WOULD I EVEN BOTHER TRYING?

Modesty is a great (often peculiarly British) quality and I find it very attractive. But this is bonkersness on a grand scale. And I know you are an intelligent woman of tall order so this is not a brainy question so much as a feelings one. You are a hostage to your feelings at times, a lot of the times. Aren't we all?

The answer is, as your brain already knows, because you are unique. There are 7.5 billion people in the world and you and I only want to work with the tiniest handful of those lovely people each, and your tiny handful and my tiny handful are not even the same. And why on earth you would bother trying is for those few people. Because of their unique and magnetic attraction to you. Because of the unique connection they will feel with you. Because of the unique work they will do with you and only you.

Stop any sense of being in competition with another living soul; it just doesn't exist. And think instead of those lovely little few you are going to love working with, and they with you. Do it for them. Do it for you. I absolutely know you will love being of service and making a difference to that one.

Now, let's go back to the head and the heart. In your head, this is a false modesty. In your weird confused-feeling heart, it isn't.

All you have to do is talk yourself out of the bonkersness and give it a go. Those lovely peeps who are just waiting for you to offer yourself to them will prove your bonkers little heart wrong. And then this one too will be consigned to the mists of time. Rock on.

Ask yourself: "What evidence do I have that my bothering to try has made a difference in my world?" Ask aloud, by all means. Write it down too. When the answers come, I hope you'll share them with me.

Remember this from Ralph Waldo Emerson: "To know even one life has breathed easier because you have lived. This is to have succeeded." A woman wrote to me this week. It was a longish message but it ended like this "So you know, I wanted to let you know you're making a difference. And thank you xxx". My work here is done (and she's not even a client!).

Do you know The Starfish Story (apologies, it is an oldie which has done the rounds a thousand times but there's a reason for that… it's also a goodie!)

Once upon a time, there was an old man who used to go to the ocean to do his writing. He had a habit of walking on the beach every morning before he began his work. Early one morning, he was walking along the shore after a big storm had passed and found the vast beach littered with starfish as far as the eye could see, stretching in both directions.

Off in the distance, the old man noticed a small boy approaching. As the boy walked, he paused every so often and as he grew closer, the man could see that he was occasionally bending down to pick up an object and throw it into the sea. The boy came closer still and the man called out, "Good morning! May I ask what it is that you are doing?"

The young boy paused, looked up, and replied "Throwing starfish into the ocean. The tide has washed them up onto the beach and they can't return to the sea by themselves," the youth replied. "When the sun gets high, they will die, unless I throw them back into the water."

The old man replied, "But there must be tens of thousands of starfish on this beach. I'm afraid you won't really be able to make much of a difference."

The boy bent down, picked up yet another starfish and threw it as far as he could into the ocean. Then he turned, smiled and said, "It made a difference to that one!"

adapted from The Star Thrower, by Loren Eiseley (1907 – 1977)

Question 11

WHY DOESN'T IT FEEL FAIR IF MY LIFE IS LOVELY?

"Other people have shit lives; it's not fair if mine is lovely."

More than anyone your questions make me want to begin with dearie, dearie me. How did you get to be so complex? It isn't clever and it isn't funny. **Stop it immediately**.

Gentle Reader, I can only speak to this woman like this because I know her well, she has a robust GSOH, she knows she's bonkers in quite a good and delightful way and some tough love is what she's after; if we were on Skype together she'd confess this and we'd laugh at that alter ego of hers. She also knows how to provide me with good questions for my book, for which I am entirely grateful.

Let's talk about a creating a lovely life first. And then fairness and what to do about it next.

Your job and my job is to create the life we want. End of.

There's no shortage of anything in this world (except as manipulated by the human race for greedy profit purposes. Not that ALL profit is wrong or bad, please note, so don't make that erroneous connection from this bracket's worth of wordiness). There's no shortage of the things we want anyway. There is a poor distribution of some things (food and money and mosquito nets mostly) and we'll come back to that in the fairness bit. And fairness is, in any event, subjective.

So go ahead and create your lovely life, *pour encourager les autres.* That's our job very definitely too. I've just enjoyed two lovely weekends back to back. I don't know that I live in loveliness all the time because into each life a little rain must fall, but I live a lovelier life than many, for sure, or at least one to my own personal taste and that's precisely the point I think. Employing myself for money is very much a part of my lovely life. Life in a job wouldn't be lovely for me at all, quite the reverse, and I packed that in pronto. So did you, my squidgy little inquisitor.

We know how to eradicate the unlovely from our lives and we have some inklings about how to insert more loveliness in its stead, so let's just crack on with that, our life's work, which you can take a lifetime to achieve if you like or you could just Get It Sorted by the end of the week. Up to you.

Today a client wrote to me to tell me a couple of work-related things she was going to achieve this week, but the bit in her email which caught my eye said: "It is lovely working in the new house this week and away from the stress of X and Y." And she added a smiley face. I replied Roger Rog to the business-y bits, as is my wont, but I bigged her up on the lovely bit because I often notice that we don't put nearly enough store by that. We are driven by the results we think we must achieve before we can have a wonderful life, whereas, in fact, it works the other way around. Happier people are more successful. Be happy first. Be happy now. Make it lovely now in any simple easy quick ways that you can.

Let me look out of my window for things to be grateful for as I write this on the day of the Great Solar Eclipse which I won't be able to see because it is in America, so I am not going to focus on that for starters. I'm focusing on the vibe, not the lack of being able to see it. Get me?

I can see lots and lots of lovely greenery and I'm not all that much of a fan of the countryside, totally urban moi. But I appreciate tall green trees with rustling leaves in the right sort of summer wind, and sometimes I can love even the rain. Of course, I am not creating either, but I am creating a lovely life if I will just choose to appreciate them. All I have to do is raise my eyes from my laptop. The more of that sort of appreciation, the better. And adding to my lovely life by thoughts and deeds and friendships and doing lots of the things I love to do (reading, writing and arithmetic, good movies and TV drama, a fantastic cup of coffee once a day, a salted caramel ice-cream on a stick) that's just a little list, makes my life lovely and ever lovelier. Sunshine is always the icing on my cake. Sunshine. Warmth and summer.

What makes your life lovely? Do more of it.

What would make your life even lovelier? Do that too.

Don't stop till you get enough.

In truth, I was just being funny. Don't stop at all because I can't look out of the window and enjoy the trees just once, that's medicine I need to keep taking daily for the rest of my natural for it to be efficacious in every way.

I'm not going to bang on (unlike you, Judith? You feeling OK?). You get what I'm on about. Go ahead and create that even lovelier life. You have my permission. Not that you need it as, to the casual observer, I know your life is pretty lovely anyway but puhleese do not put any limits on it because it's not fair. The sky's the limit when it comes to loveliness, for you and for everyone. You read these terrifically inspiring stories online about people who thrive through appalling circumstances which would finish us softies off, perhaps. But who knows? Perhaps tough times would be the making of us too?

Fairness now. There's plenty of that to go around as well. In a certain light we do run the risk of sounding like the people on Overheard in Waitrose, I mean "But what about the poor people, Dahling?" And I think what we do either before, during or after the creation of our own loveliness, is we work out how we want to contribute to fairness with our effort, or our money, or our time, or our gifts, or our fundraising, or cake-baking, or marching on Westminster, or our volunteering in the third world or operating on poorly people in war zones, or whatever. Whatever we do to redress unfairness must also contribute to the loveliness, by which I mean I must make us feel better about ourselves and the world around us knowing we have done our bit in a way which is meaningful and satisfying. Do-gooding is one of the best things I have ever done when my life was low.

I've written to my MP today, coincidentally. About a terrible social injustice that's going on right now in my life. It is impacting a lot of women my age, but would it even have flitted across my radar if I hadn't been slap bang in the middle of the catchment for it? I doubt it. I choose my battles wisely. Personally, I am not so highly motivated as I know you are to make a Big Difference in the world. I content myself with helping those who want to do that. I focus on the ones I can help and I let them go forth and multiply with it. To me, it is the same difference and it is a distinction I joined up the dots to make when working with a lot of the entrepreneurs in Roger Hamilton's Wealth Dynamics community. They are planet-changers. I am not. But I made a difference to that one and it gladdens my heart to know that one will go forth and amplify our work together to make their own life lovelier AND the lives of others. It is enough for me. It is more than enough. One at a time, Sweet Jesus. One at a time. The ripples spread outwards.

Here's my tip. Contribute to the fixing of what you can. Don't take on all causes. I have two right now. Don't take on everything, unless that would constitute a lovely life for you. Causes and dwelling on the awfulness in the world tend to make my life less lovely and how is that serving anyone? You know I do good. I know you do good. We have to trust that we do enough and if we do not, then we can simply up our game anytime we can find or raise capacity for that.

Just like self-employment, our efforts at making the world a fairer place are better if they are directed, targeted at fewer areas, those that are really important to us like say homelessness or hunger. Which reminds me that those are the sorts of things which John-Paul Flintoff taught me start at home. If you have an abundance of apples which have fallen from your tree, put them in a basket and knock on your neighbour's door with your children and offer them apples. They think you are weird on your own, but they feel happy and safe when it's you and your kids. All these problems need sorting right where we live, not necessarily in the third world, and it fosters community which is definitely a loveliness enhancer.

Over to you now, Beloved.

NOTES

- What would make your life (even) lovelier?
- When did you last make time for that?
- How can you schedule in your regular tree medicine?

Find out more about John-Paul Flintoff at his website: http://www.flintoff.org/

Question 12

WHAT IF IT DOESN'T GO TO PLAN AGAIN?

"A lot of people are afraid because they have never tried anything different. My fear comes from having tried and it didn't go to plan."

What your question reminds me of is what they say in the financial world of investments:

Past performance is no guarantee (or even indication) of future results.

My first ever personal development book and one which would still be in my top 10 is Feel the Fear and Do It Anyway by Susan Jeffers and it is still the only antidote to fear, that ghost who visits me in the night but tends to disappear again in the daytime when I feel like I can do something about my nameless dreads. Or when the full glare of daylight enables me to see them for the spectres they are.

I'm writing elsewhere in this book about fear for it is a recurring theme. I don't think it ever goes away. Yes, you meet fearless people. But I'm not sure I'd want to be fearless, would you? I think there are some things it is healthy to be fearful of - sharks, snakes, texting while driving, going too near the edge on the top of a very tall building which doesn't have appropriate safety barriers in place. Those fears are how I keep myself alive, I respect them.

There are a couple of things I'm fearful of (skiing, for starters) and at least one thing I wasn't fearful enough of (the big waves at a beach on my favourite Caribbean island that took one of my nine lives and is still the stuff of nightmares).

What we don't want to do is to become fearful of everything. And I can see how one or more bad experience, of the sort I know you have had, might make you more fearful that your next Big Gamble won't pay off either. But hey, it's a life and, as my brother always says, life is a dangerous sport. That's if you play it right. That's how we know we are alive, fully alive, not living a half-life.

When it comes to fears, by the way, if you have a logical brain and this wouldn't frighten you too much, there's a book I remember enjoying a lot called Risk: The Science and Politics of Fear by Dan Gardner in which he teaches that we are frightened of all the wrong things. We should be frightened of diabetes but we are not, we are frightened of heart disease and cancer. We should be frightened of driving a car, but we are not, we are frightened of flying. We get it all upside down. Things that are risky don't appear so to us. Things that aren't, do. Go figure. We are illogical creatures basically, or we simply haven't studied enough science or stats.

Your concerns appear well-founded. One big bad experience (and some small ones too) does tend to put you off a bit and start to worry you more (than when you were younger and less concerned) about "getting it right" next time. But with your previous adventure, you did rather rashly jump off the metaphorical cliff. With your biz, it'll be much gentler and you'll be able to tweak as you go. There are ways you can protect yourself and make it feel safe for as long as you need that. Think of it like training wheels on your bike.

Here's a final thought. How about re-framing fear to uncertainty? Uncertainty is a given with self-employment. It is something we adapt to, it becomes our new normal and, in the end, it feels good. Risks can be quantified and we can break them down into smaller ones if you feel you need to. I don't think you will. You've learned from your Big Bad One, that's what we are supposed to do. This time will go more easily and you will be fine either way, Brave Bird that you are. And this time I'm going to be here with you. And two always makes it feel easier, don't you think? We're in this together.

These are feelings. They are giving you useful feedback. And you can thank them for those messages and re-interpret them. Just because your Mum says you are to be careful before crossing the road, doesn't mean she expects you to get run over. Take care, that's all. Take care.

Feel the Fear And Do It Anyway: How to Turn Your Fear and Indecision into Confidence and Action by Susan Jeffers

Risk: The Science and Politics of Fear by Dan Gardner

Question 13

HOW CAN NICE GIRLS DO NASTY THINGS?

Some of my clients' problems are like buses. Three come along at once. And this question is a fabulous example of that.

Three separate clients and colleagues (two teams led by women, and one by a man, so this isn't a female thing, it's a niceness thing) are grappling with matters arising from one "troublemaker" on staff. That person doesn't even need to be causing orthodox trouble. But what they **are** doing is unsettling the team and using up inordinate amounts of everyone's time and psychic energy while we all work out what to do about them. One of my clients has recently given me a good name for these people - chi-bandits!

And we've known all along what to do - we have to get rid - we just don't want to do it, because we are nice. And because we like and respect parts of the person and because the person has many strengths we appreciate, and it feels mean. But they just aren't fitting into our team, and everyone else feels bad. And the problem person starts to be at the root of every problem our business has.

I've known people like this in my life too, where I have allowed the fact that they were disruptive to be overlooked by my kind reasoning that there wasn't a nasty bone in their body, or they'd been so kind to me that time I was in a spot, or that I owe them something or some bonkersness to stop me doing what needs to be done. I need to distance myself from them for my sanity.

And so it is with these three business examples.

What they all have in common is that there's something "wrong" with the person's energy/work/role/influence/results in our business, or lack thereof, but because we like or feel sorry for the person we put off and off doing the dirty deed, and the longer we put it off the harder it is and the more disruptive the cuckoo becomes in the nest. And the more powerful and manipulative, even passive-aggressively or apparently unknowingly. Yeah, right.

We wring our hands, we are so grateful to them for X and Y and Z, but what we really need them to do is A and B and C and they are not getting it. Yes, we've already had the full and frank exchange of views conversation, more than once.

They need special treatment. They are highly emotional divas (say) and we have to continually take them out for a special treat and calm them down and then everything's fine and dandy for a few days until the next episode. We are hostage to their emotional roller-coasters again when what we want at work is calm and efficiency.

Or they are in sales and haven't sold anything for a year and that's really what we need them to do for our business and they are not doing it and we carry them because they have other strengths, they send out the newsletter for us or some such silly task that anyone could do for us. We are just justifying our own niceness or weakness in that we haven't done what we know needs to be done.

In all examples, there is a terrible waste of time and emotion while we **endlessly** debate how we feel and why we are putting off what we know needs to be done. That's why we all do so much wittering about it because this doesn't make sense and it never will. Some things cannot be fixed or understood. Sometimes they just need to end a.s.a.p. to stop the bleeding.

It is so easy for me to spot this because I am not a member of your team. So when you describe this problem and we decide what we are going to do (eventually) and then we go onto your next problem, the same problem underlies it and always will until you Do The Deed.

CHOP!

I sound terribly brutal, and I know you've already read enough of this book to know that I am not. But I know when your business is being threatened by a troublemaker, whether or not that's their intent and mainly it isn't. And I know when you are being held hostage to emotions, the emotions of that person, the fears you have about how they will feel if you sack them, and the roiling emotions of all the unsettled members of the rest of your team who rotate between outrage against said person and sympathy for her/him.

We are all too nice for our own good. And deep down everyone knows the truth of what has to happen, perhaps especially the troublemaker.

Trouble troublemaker, it's your middle name. You cause some sort of drama wherever you go. And we are grateful to you for bringing your special brand of troublemaking to our door so that we can learn to do what must be done to protect our business, our sanity and the well-being of the other members of our team.

And now we release you back into the wilds of the employment market. Go with our love.

Oh, this has happened to you before? This keeps happening? Well, I never. Soon you'll learn, then.

Look! People are strange and interesting and complex, and some of us are bonkers in a good way. And others are bonkers in a way which we don't have time to fix during office hours, nor should we. When you dispense with his/her services, he/she won't die. They'll do what we all do when we've been sacked. We find another job or another way of getting our bills paid. **And that is not and never has been and never will be your responsibility.**

You are probably not A Boss until you have sacked someone or laid someone off. It can be brutal but it must be done to protect the vital life force of what you are creating. Think of the bigger picture and steel yourself to do what must be done. TM won't be surprised. It happens to her all the time. But this is her opportunity to get a grip and go perhaps to a larger employer where this behaviour is simply not tolerated and where she'll get that vibe from Day One and she won't be trying it on with them. Looking at it like that, you are doing her a favour.

Go do her a favour today.

The One-Minute Manager by Kenneth Blanchard and Spencer Johnson which teaches how to manage staff with One Minute Goals, One Minute Praisings and One Minute Reprimands. It is a very thin book at just 112 pages and an easily-read story you'll never forget. If you find these staffing issues recurring, read the book again as often as you need.

Question 14

HOW CAN I STEP UP TO A BIGGER GAME WITHOUT FEELING EXPOSED?

What if exposure isn't what it takes, just visibility?

My client who offered this conundrum is on the cusp of playing bigger. She is a woman who has more than enough capacity for that. She has capacity in bucketfuls. Her capacity is full to overflowing. We all have this. We all have the capacity to be extraordinary if we choose.

Her anxiety is around feeling exposed.

This is just a re-frame opportunity. You need never do anything you don't want to do. OK, you might choose to do some things that stretch you a bit, outside the old CZ (comfort zone, hate that jargon but it had to be said here). But you need never do anything that feels exposing.

If you are called to play a bigger game, and she is, then she may need to blow her own trumpet some more or find ways to get the brass section to make a big noise on her behalf. And people will see her. But she is already quite highly visible in a couple of areas of her life. She writes about one of her passions as a Proper Writer and she's published for that and shares it all on social media and if she feels any compunction about that she's never shared it with me.

She also has a day job where she's effortlessly competent and in high demand for her particular skills which pay the bills (and then some) and provides a lot of interest, satisfaction and global adventures. She's visible there too, otherwise she wouldn't get offered those contracts.

But there is a third area of her life and work where the stepping up comes in. She isn't as visible there yet as she is in the other two, but the very fact that she is comfortable with her visibility in the other two areas means she knows how this feels in her areas of competence, she doesn't yet know how it feels around her passion where perhaps, for now, she feels more vulnerable. Maybe this one is The Big One, the one that really counts?

I know by the way my client told me this story that she secretly wants to do this because she is quite Starry*.

I remember saying on my 60th birthday a couple of years ago that I thought I would do more public speaking. I didn't really want to do it, I just thought I should, could, might. I haven't yet but I don't rule it out. It doesn't feel like exposing myself because I've done enough to know it will be OK, and anyway my speaking is never about me, it's about you and I love that. But this does feel the same to me. Like the whole next level of visibility and I am always in two minds about that.

We all have a marker in the sand where on one side it's safe and comforting and on the other side it's a bit scary for now, but we know (secretly) we want to go there.

Go there. And always remember your personal power. Be prepared for the stretch but there's never any need to show anything you don't want to be seen. You keep that power even when standing on bigger and bigger stages. No one can make you do anything you don't want to do, that's non-negotiable. It is safe for you to do this. And you will love it. And I already know you'll be great. And so do you.

NOTES

Fear of Being Seen - Tapping with Brad Yates:
https://www.youtube.com/watch?v=XJjadWI_CSk

If you don't yet know anything about EFT (Emotional Freedom Technique) also known as tapping, start with Brad's intro video:
https://www.youtube.com/watch?v=JiD72cZ5mcU

Brad has a quick video for almost every emotion from which you would like to be free.

Question 15

HOW CAN I LESSEN THE FEELINGS OF UTTER CHAOS?

Towards the end of the summer term, a client of mine confessed to feeling "utterly chaotic". Don't all mothers feel like that at the end of term? Aren't we all hanging on to get as much of our work done alongside all the other duties and responsibilities in our lives and businesses, especially if we know we are going to switch off for a couple of months to be with the kids?

Chaotic doesn't feel nice, I know.

When I was an accountant, December was our chaotic month; not January, that's for tax accountants in the UK. We had to do 31 days' work in 21 days and go to all our clients' Christmas parties as well, and cope with their disappointment if we couldn't due to pressure of work. And, if we did make it to some or all of the clients' Christmas shindigs and to all of our own parties as well, some of us would be turning up at work feeling either tired or hungover or both. That is one of the worst ways to start your own holidays I can recall, and we'd usually fall ill during our own eventual time off. The self-employed Christmas bug, I suspect you've had a visit or two from that one?

It was perfectly normal for my staff, the majority of whom were mothers, to be doing the Christmas payroll for our clients on Christmas Eve. And you know how important the December payroll is because it includes everyone's Christmas bonuses and no-one can pay their bills for the festive season without their enhanced pay. Was it our fault we were working on Christmas Eve? Aren't you thinking… "You, Judith? The great Morganiser? You couldn't order things better than that? You had your staff working on the afternoon of 24th December?"

I, for instance, am the woman who did the payroll on 9/11 because 9th September was a Tuesday that year. And in 2001 we used to use BACS for paying salaries which took three days. And although the entirety of the rest of my client's office staff was sitting in the boardroom watching the TV and processing their emotions, I was not. I was doing the payroll because I knew that, by Friday, they'd still all want their pay even if, and especially if, the world was coming to an end.

But the Christmas chaos was outside our control. It was the blankety-blank clients. Although we pestered and cajoled and encouraged them to get themselves organised ahead of time, they seemed unable to do that. And it felt utterly chaotic to us and for us. So this resonates, very much. The word chaos puts me in mind of it being created by another, outside my control. I am not one who creates her own chaos, generally speaking, though I have known people who do that, oh yes siree. God help us all.

But here's how I think about it. Some times are chaotic and that's OK because we know the chaos must and will soon end.

It's chaos all the time which is utterly debilitating and must be ordered and organised so that you don't dwell in chaos, 'cos that'll do for you faster than you can say knife. You'll be living on adrenaline which inexorably leads to burnout. Don't do that. **Stop it immediately.**

So allow for the fact that at times, for perfectly logical reasons, many of which are entirely outside your control, you will be and/or feel utterly chaotic. It gladdens my heart that you don't like it because this will encourage you to do all you can to ensure it isn't so bad next time, easier the time after that and eventually it doesn't occur nearly so much, if at all.

As the kids grow up it becomes less chaotic in that way. Another form of chaos enters your life altogether but you have slightly more control over the degree to which you get sucked into teenage chaos than you do the chaos caused by tinies, who want you to watch their every sack race, nativity play and egg hunt. But aah! Why wouldn't you want to be there anyway, despite the biz and other knock-on chaos it causes? And just think about those poor folks who have to ask for time off from a J.O.B. and may not even be able to attend at all.

We are so lucky in our choice of employing ourselves for money. Chaotic it may be at times, but is chaos mostly of our own choosing.

We can always (or nearly always) do something about the feelings we don't like feeling, even if all we do is to change how we choose to think about such things.

This week an example of this occurred when I was doing my own accounts. My first thought was "Isn't it a bummer that PayPal takes such a hefty chunk out of my income?" My second thought was "Isn't it wonderful that I am able to trade with people all over the world with such effortless ease, so much so that money can come in while I am sleeping, thanks to PayPal?" And then it don't seem so bad, as Julie Andrews might so easily say, or sing.

How can your utter chaos be OK and philosophically incorporated into a reasonably balanced life?

Well for starters, I'd be doing a lot more breathing. And a lot more planning. And then I'd be telling myself I'm so lucky to have such beautiful children and a great toptastic reason not to be working today and how these moments are so soon gone and turned into memories which fade. What's important is Being There. Now. Fully present. Which means not looking at your mobile phone to see what's going on at work because you've planned it thus and anyway, those grown-up children who are your clients can manage their own emotions while you stand proudly by on the edge of sports day or even, for all I know, take part in the Mothers' Egg and Spoon. Go for it!

Honestly? Don't bother going if you are just going to look at your mobile phone. Your kids know they don't have your full attention and that feels just awful. Keeping your attention on just one thing is the fastest way I know to bring you out of chaos and into the joy of the present moment.

A therapist said something very useful to me once about feelings of chaos just before a holiday. She said: "You don't need to organise your WHOLE life just because you are going on holiday" which is something those of us who love control tend to try and achieve. Impossible!

And then I found this gorgeous quote for you. There are so many gorgeous thoughts about chaos it was hard to choose - do spend a little time on that yourself to see if you can find your own personal favourite. Here, for now, is mine:

"You need chaos within you to give birth to a dancing star."
Friedrich Nietzsche

You are SO giving birth to your dancing star!

Question 16

WHY WOULD ANYONE WANT TO BUY MY STUFF?

"Nobody will want to buy my artwork when there is so much choice out there."

Ooh, I've got another client talking to me along these same lines right now.

My favourite stat in answer to this question, you'll remember, is that there are about 7.5 billion people in the world. That's a lot. And as a coach, I only need about 100 of those a year to make a cracking living in My Biz My Way.

Yes, there's a lot of art in the world, but there are a lot of business coaches too. And this is an entirely good thing, because between us we have to serve 7.5 billion people and we sure can't do that single-handedly, nor do we want to.

People love choice. They want all of the colours in all of the sizes to quote that wonderful old BT advert starring Maureen Lipman and Richard Wilson, remember?

Some of the 7.5bn people will be drawn to your artwork and some not, just as some are drawn to me as their business coach and some not.

Some will. Some won't. So what?

Don't take it personally. It isn't personal, though I know it often feels quite painful or has that propensity. We all toughen up in the end. Don't take too long over that. Adopt an approach of abundance. Wonderful if they do, wonderful if they don't. And, of course, just because they don't today, doesn't mean they won't double back later. Once seen, never forgotten. Or at least never forgotten by your ideal clients and customers.

If you look back over the people who have loved (and preferably bought) your artwork, what did they love about it even if you've only ever had one sale? If that person or those people told you what they loved about your arty stuff, there's your proof that your buyers do exist. There is perhaps a clue to what "they" call your ideal customer (a concept I don't wholly buy into, by the way, but we'll talk more about that anon).

Your first few sales prove the concept. You can create something that others want to buy.

After that, your job is to create as much and as freely and as beautifully as you want, and to get it out into the world.

People who love arty stuff buy arty stuff. But they can't buy your arty stuff unless they know about it.

So the plan is:

1. Create art
2. Show the buyers of the world what you've got
3. Create desire for your arty stuff
4. Allow fans to buy

Simple!

Real collectors who love art love choice. They have stuff by all sorts of different artists covering every inch of their walls. That would do my head in. I'd rather have just one significant piece I loved every day. But I am not normal in this regard (nor many others either!).

But I've bought pictures to put on my walls and other arty stuff like pots because I came across them, I loved them, and I put my hand in my pocket. It never occurred to me to shop around and search the world in case there was something out there that was better or even more to my taste though no doubt that is some people's operating system. We are not all the same, remember. I bought on impulse, because I liked it, because I was feeling like a little retail therapy that day. That are gazillions of reasons why people buy. Let's just leave that bit to them, it's not our job. Creating is our job.

Collectors would, if necessary, sell or archive one piece of artwork in order to put another on display if they even think thoughts about liking one "better".

Choice is good. And I know that you know that when you allow this thought in your question, you are sliding into scarcity and thoughts of competition. There is no competition for what you do because you are unique, as am I. You are possibly also hiding, and using this for a cover as to why you are not making your artwork more visible and more available. You could be "blaming" choice.

Make art. Show art. Sell art. Create and fully enjoy Your Arty Biz Your Way.

NOTES

- **In what ways do you appreciate choice in your life, and as a buyer of anything?**
- **How does that help you now to better understand those who will buy from you?**

Question 17

WILL MY EFFORTS RESULT IN MY BECOMING A BAG LADY?

"The overwhelming 'bag lady' scenario that screeches into panoramic view whenever an idea that stretches me appears."

OK, let me see if I get this one. The overwhelming bag lady scenario only screeches into view with a stretchy idea, but not with easier ones?

That is a form of delicious bonkersness, of course. Thank you!

I have been prey myself to the bag lady thing, on occasion. We all are. So what I and my self-employed pals do is go into it, explore it, see what it would be like and what might happen.

If you ended up in a cardboard box, who would offer you shelter?

I have a family. I wouldn't want to prevail upon them, but I would in those circumstances and they certainly wouldn't want a bag lady for a sister/aunt, but that is an option. I have friends with houses with spare bedrooms, some with even more than one home. I wouldn't want to prevail upon them either but I could. "Could I come and stay in your spare room for (say) a month or three?" You could line up a few of those I dare say, which might give you as much as a year to get back on your feet and - let's face it - this isn't going to happen anyway, is it? But I do think it is useful asking yourself a series of What If questions for any fearful scenario. In that way, you can both bust through the bonkersness and reassure yourself that you DO have options. There are even places that genteel women such as ourselves can go and take up residence if we find ourselves distressed at any point in our lives. Communes where you volunteer in return for board and lodging. Somewhere you can make a contribution. Anyway, I'm not going to bang on about these because I know it's not a serious question in that way.

It's more about the idea that stretches you. Why do those have special powers of terror, I wonder? And why are you giving those ones the big screen panoramic treatment?

You are so very inventive in your rich fantasy life, I wonder if you have missed your vocation? Only joking! The last thing we need right now is a change of vocation. [Dear God, close one there, Judith!]

We need ways of calming your anxieties and hallucinations. Breathing. Knowing that everything is alright really because it always has been and it always will be.

Tell you what... I am wondering if one of the big stretchy ideas isn't precisely The One you should be running with instead of a series of much smaller ones which tie you up in busyness?

And, honestly, when it comes to Bag Ladies, you are absolutely my favourite.

Exercise: Feel into the worst case scenario.

- **What options do you have, pre-cardboard box?**
- **How resourceful could you be if your back was truly to the wall?**
- **Do you need a Plan B?**
- **If so, what is it?**

Question 18

WHY DO I LIVE IN ENDLESS FEAR?

"The endless fear that any idea, no matter how noble and/or amazing, will never generate enough money to support me."

Endless fear just goes with the territory of self-employment. Until you adapt. Until it becomes your new normal. Until you no longer notice. Be brave, me hearty. You can do this. Avast!

However, as you embrace those fears, I don't want them to do internal damage, I want them to embolden you. I want you to bust through them and stand on them to tackle the next one.

I am careful to point out here that this isn't all there is. I know you know this already. Life's rich tapestry has fearful bits, but it isn't just The NeverEnding Story of Fear.

I am wondering what things you've done in your life that you feared and which, when it came to mastering them, made you feel wonderful, exhilarated, all-conquering?

I have a friend who is quite fearful in some elements of her real life but endlessly brave when it comes to plank-breaking, wing-walking, and jumping off Turkish mountains strapped to a complete stranger and a foreigner with no shared language to boot! These are personal development metaphors, aren't they? And the hope is that the bravery will translate into your real life.

Conversely, I don't do any of those things, I'm a bit of a physical coward, and yet I feel quite brave in my choice of employing myself for money. I am more up for the reality than the metaphor. I live the bravery every day, but I don't enjoy volunteering for it on my holidays. I prefer to sit under a tree, in a pretty frock, and entertain myself with the view and an ice-lolly while I wait for her to come back down to earth. And she can take as long as she likes, for I am content. Each to their own.

I bet you've done some brave things in your life. I know you have, you are a Brit living in another country for starters. That must have taken some bravery? How did you do that?

One of my colleagues is on a mission right now, accidentally or on purpose, to become less fearful and I can report that it is working.

I think what we must do with fears is say "BOO!" to them and watch them vanish.

As a single woman, I have dealt with a lot of scary things in my life where I didn't have the luxury of someone to do it for me while I stood on a chair. If it's only you, you have to deal with birds in the house, spiders, rats, pigeon fleas, snails coming out of the under the sink cupboard in the kitchen because the floor wasn't finished properly etc. The list often seems to go on and on.

You've had babies too I think. Gosh! Does anything take any more bravery than that? Not in my world! And yet you took it in your stride.

So we know you are a brave woman.

OK, you are not yet brave enough to believe that your noble and amazing ideas will support you, and yet I know you have been supporting yourself for quite a while. There does seem to be some recurring theme about the bigger, the stretchier, the more noble and amazing your ideas are, the less likely they are to work and that's my kind of bonkersness. Thanks so much for bringing that one to this book. The readers will love you for that one and resonate very much.

The only thing you can do is prove yourself wrong. Feel the fear and do it anyway. Bust through it. Give the lie to fear.

They say the opposite of fear and its antidote is love. How could you love one of your noble and amazing ideas enough to allow it to make money for you easily and effortlessly? I'll just leave it there. There's your opportunity.

PS I LOVE noble and amazing. Crack on, Braveheart!

Ask yourself: "What would a BRAVE woman do?"

Thanks for that one to the woman I am proud to call my friend, Marion Ryan.

BREATHING SPACE – CHAPTER TWO - FEELINGS

Chapter Two is all about feelings of uncertainty, self-doubt, fairness, exposure, chaos, niceness, nastiness, fear, fear and more fear.

Did you spot any of your own demons in there? Which ones? And what will you do to bust through them now, or learn to live with and love their helpful little warnings to you? The game here is to be aware of your neuroses, downplay what you consider to be your weaknesses and carry on regardless knowing you are good enough and that those struggly parts of yourself can peacefully co-exist with the you that is the emerging biz owner.

What struck you as bonkersness in others, issues you simply do not have? Hurrah! Take some time now to think about your strengths and playing to them when you employ yourself for money. What would that change for you? Isn't it great to know that we can feel all these emotions (if we want to) and yet still employ ourselves for money, and that there's nothing wrong with us? These feelings are human and normal, though there's no need to lay claim to all of them by any means, I don't want this book to introduce you to new forms of hitherto unknown bonkersness and infect you with it!

Let's start from the place that everything is perfect, just exactly as it is, including you. And that life is also incomprehensibly perfect. I know you know that, whatever's taken place in your past or still shadows you to this day. Our demons do not own or diminish us.

The opportunity here is to surrender the struggle and to stop defining yourself by it. If you are one of those who says "what I struggle with is…", what would you choose to say to me instead now?

"I am aware that sometimes I am susceptible to feelings of X, Y and Z and that I have a way to love and accept them and move forward anyway..." - IN YOUR OWN WORDS PLEASE!

To feel is human. Let's celebrate that. Let's start to see problems as opportunities. Let's start by listing and leveraging your strengths.

Use this space to write down any thoughts about feelings both helpful and unhelpful which come to you. And if all you can think of are perceived weaknesses and struggle, what are the compensations of those? What do people who love you say about you? What would I appreciate about you?

CHAPTER THREE

Financial

Question 19

COULDN'T I JUST HELP PEOPLE FOR FREE?

"Asking people for money is all a bit icky, and it would be much better all round if I could just help people for free."

Oh, I think this is my favourite one of yours so far!

And I believe it comes from most of us having begun life in the world of work by having a job. There you don't have to ask people for money. The unmentionable reason we are all there, toiling away at our workstations, is that we will be paid at the end of the week or month. We don't ask for it, it is directly credited to our bank account.

You did ask for it, but in oblique polite ways like applying for a job, attending an interview, getting the job, and turning up clean and tidy and on time for 9-5.30 five days a week throughout the month. And in return for that "asking", you were paid money.

When you employ yourself for money, you do have to ask other people for money, yes. But there are gazillions of ways of doing this subtly, and elegantly and even in-yer-face ways and they are perfectly normal and we see them going on around us all day long and we don't turn a hair.

We know what lots of things cost and how we are expected to pay for them, and we are totally cool with that as a purchaser. We are invited to buy something, a product or a service, for money. And we make up our minds whether or not we want it and how much we want it and how much we are prepared to pay for it, and we whip out a credit card or cash.

So far so normal.

Why then is it any different the other way around? How can you take all your icky feelings out of it? Nobody on the purchasing ends feels this, by the way, it's you injecting all the ick into it.

You have to take the anxiety and desperation out of the whole thang.

Get advice from someone like me about how to price what you offer. Do not make the mistake of starting too low as that **is** icky and impossible to rectify. Do charge what you are worth and be abundant about it - lay out your stall, offer your potential client or customer a range of what you offer, create desire and offer them easy ways to pay, both online and off, but preferably on or at least digital.

Be equally happy if they say either no, or no not now, or no not ever.

If they do say no, you are then available to someone who will say yes, just like you in a shoe shop. Just because you say no today doesn't mean you won't buy shoes tomorrow, that there's anything wrong with the shoes or that the vendor has outrageous chutzpah in asking for money for his shoes.

It just means you are not ready to open up your wallet today. But you might be back.

And if the shoes are lovely and you need or want shoes and they've stolen your heart, one day soon you will be ready and the vendor will still be there, ready and willing to accept your money although you might not get those particular shoes unless you make up your mind to purchase while they are still in the shop. Always a risk with shoes, innit? And so it is too with whatever you are selling. We small biz owners do not have infinite capacity.

And yet there need be no scarcity here, on either side of this transaction. The world is full of stuff (and shoes) and people offering a full panoply of treats and essentials to us. The choice is always ours about what we want to buy, when we need it and what we are willing to pay for it.

This is how the world goes around.

Look at the things you buy, how you shop and how you like spending money and what things you like to buy with it. Is that icky on this side of the exchange? No! So why does it suddenly become so when things are reversed?

You buy what you want easily and the same applies when it comes to people paying you for your stuff. No biggie. Chillax (used ironically, obvs).

In terms of it being much better all round if you could just help people for free, trust me that's wrong too. It is a generally accepted principle that people do not value what they either get for free or which is too cheap. I for one don't want much for free, am not interested in bargains or discounts or cheapness. I am not saying that's the way to be, it is the way I am and mostly that's a choice. I have occasionally bagged the odd bargain and been chuffed for that, but I don't go out of my way to hunt them down. And I am by no means alone in this. Cheap or free is not attractive to me. I am more than happy to pay whatever a commodity is worth to me, almost always the going rate.

If you can be persuaded to align yourself with charging properly for your glorious talents then you will have loads of money and you will be able to make donations, be a philanthropist, and give away whatever you like.

Put your oxygen mask on first. Make yourself strong. Then look after those, if any, who need your charity, donations and philanthropy.

Read the Huffpo explanation for why we must put on our own oxygen mask first: https://tinyurl.com/HuffpoOxygenMask

Question 20

HOW CAN PITCHING FOR WORK BE EASIER?

The key to pitching for work is equanimity. Calmness and composure especially in a difficult situation. That's what the dictionary says. But who says pitching is a difficult situation?

Well, my clients do tend to find it fraught with potential pitfalls. Their initial inclination is to go in far too cheap to get the work. Their erroneous assumption is that everyone wants everything for cheap. This isn't so, and that's a lesson I learned when I owned a travel agency in my late thirties and my assistant was in her twenties because we wanted our travel for the best possible bargain prices always, to match our budget at that stage of our lives. But it became abundantly clear very quickly that wasn't the case with our somewhat more affluent clients, even those who looked very much like us.

Some people like a little bit or even quite a lot of luxury on their holidays and they've saved up for it, or they don't have to.

So, firstly… never assume.

Secondly, don't pitch in your reality. Pitch in the reality of your client.

I always like to know how much my clients are earning so I know their financial reality. If they are earning £200 an hour in their work, why would I accept (or they pay me) anything less? There are many people who don't penny-pinch whatever their financial reality, and many others who always ask for a discount because.

But the key to pitching is twofold.

1. Pitch your work at a price you would be absolutely delighted to do the work for, even if you charge other clients more. It's harder to charge the same client more next time as you set a precedent with your first job, which is just one of the reasons not to undercharge them because assumptions can be made. Of course, if you decide to do that just to get the

work, then you must make abundantly clear (and ensure your client understands and retains this point particularly, don't gloss over it because you are embarrassed to talk about money) your reason for doing that. For instance, you always do the first one at a discounted rate of X but your usual charges are Y and the concrete mutual understanding and acknowledgment is that it will definitely be Y next time, no questions asked. The awful thing when you do it for X and that's cheap and you are consequently phenomenally good value for money is that your delighted client will make referrals to people, all of whom will want your heavily discounted price. Don't do it. BUT, if you do, for any reason, never quote a price that would make you miserable while doing the work. There is nothing like being overworked and underpaid. Remember how that felt in a JOB? Yep, that's why we left. We are not going to replicate that exact same broken dynamic out here on the outside. So pitch, get the work at a price that delights you even if slightly less than you want to be charging, explain your reasons for doing that THIS TIME, and thoroughly love doing the work with a high vibe that leaks from every pore. Even if lessons are learned, about pricing or anything, your client doesn't need to know that. Stay in abundance always.

2. If they do not accept your quote for any reason, be absolutely delighted about that too. Great if they do, great if they don't. How is not winning the pitch good, Judith? Well, it keeps you free for the right client, and they weren't the right client, they were the wrong one. No skin off your nose. Plenty more fish in the Sea of Clients. Keep on with the keeping on, the right one's just around the next bend (rock?) and is going to be so much more delightful to work with, in every way.

Charge a fee you are going to be delighted to do the work for.
Be equally happy whether or not you get the work.
There's no room for scarcity in this pricing game. I think I can teach you that, and if you follow these principles you can teach yourself that too.

When I was an accountant and I felt my business at times to be either full up or faced with a client I didn't want to work with, I would double or even treble my prices and they would still buy! It is almost never about the price however much we think it is, however skint and scarce our own financial reality right now. So here's my best advice for you. Double the price and half the number of clients, that's where we're headed with this sort of thinking. Try that one on and let me know how it feels.

One of my clients, the brilliant Sam, always asks: "What's the brief and what's your budget?" Then hold your breath and say nothing until they answer those questions. Then you say that you will get back to them with what you can do within their budget by close of business Friday, or whatever timescale you both agree. Buy yourself time to think about it and, if you need, get onto a call with me pronto. Or Ask Judith in the Facebook group and we'll help you stand your ground.

One of my colleagues taught me what they say in the film industry, which is "Do you want it good, or do you want it Thursday?" meaning good or fast? You can't always have both. Your equivalent question might be "Do you want it good, or cheap?" although I wouldn't be putting that idea in their minds, frankly. You might even turn away those who want it cheap, unless your business specialises in cheap. I hope your business doesn't specialise in cheap. That doesn't lead to a lovely business unless you are piling it high, and in that instance then turnover is the name of your game and you really need to be Tesco to make money at that and even then, it's a very risky and complex strategy which is out of our league.

Question 21

WHAT'S THE BEST WAY TO DISCOUNT?

Very much related to pitching is discounting, and I touched on how to do it there too.

You discount, if you do it at all, for a reason. And you discount visibly. So potential clients know now and also in future what you charge and they can internalise that and when they return, if you don't have a special on, they pay your going rate.

Reasons to discount include (but are not limited to) helping your client make up their mind to buy at this price and to buy within your time frame. Usually now or, at the least, very quickly. So you help clients to buy by offering a discount by a certain deadline. These are perfectly normal marketing techniques. If you don't like them, don't do them. But do notice how often they have helped you to make a purchasing decision in the past.

Clients know how often I say "sell as you buy." If you are someone who buys because time's running out or because there's limited availability and you fear you are about to miss out, or because you want to grab this bargain price while it's still a limited time only offer, then sell like that too.

I was surprised and delighted to note recently that a little rush of new clients had all bought a year's membership of my top-priced coaching Club 100, happy to pay for 1-2-1 privacy and the luxury personal -v- group attention, and they all paid in advance; not money no object, but easy access to funds for whatever they want.

No discounts were offered. But on another occasion I might do that, or bundle in a bonus, a delicious little cherry on the top of my sales cake.

When talking to clients I always help them to find a good reason why they might discount if they are feeling the knock down vibe. So long as your client knows the full price and, more importantly, the full **value** of your offer, then fine by me. The full value of your offer is important, no it's vital.

Even if they are getting your product or service for say £1,000 where normally you charge £1,500, you very definitely want them to know they are getting something with a value of £1,500 and for them to treat it with due respect.

People value highly priced things and respect them more which means they get more enjoyment out of them. Weird, but there you go.

Here's a little snippet of a question/observation which came in for a client for this book. As you will see, it is very much on topic here.

"My issue this week was to do with mindset on negotiating a day rate. My assumption/unfounded thought was that if I don't say yes to what the client wants in terms of rate they'll a) be angry with me and/or b) say 'forget it'. Not thinking that actually c) they might respect me more for holding my ground and realising my worth!"

And I replied (er...I am not sure I did send this in reply so much as just thought it).

"This is gorgeous. Thanks for offering it up for the book, and big congrats on noticing it. I think if we get quiet enough we can recognise bonkers thoughts like these for what they are, hallucinations as my coach calls them, we make them up, they aren't true. However, how many of us (except us single introverts) take the time or create the opportunity to get quiet enough?"

In summary, don't rush to discount. Think it through. Many people ask for a discount "because", a reason they have simply invented because they love to haggle. That doesn't mean you have to give it to them, especially if you have already cut your margins to the bone. Think about whether you could do your best work at the discounted price under discussion, or whether you would feel grumpy and underpaid and on the back foot all the way through the work. That's most undesirable, especially if it's a long contract. And look! As my client says, they might respect you more for holding your ground and realising your worth.

I know. Unbelievable, isn't it?

Believe it.

NOTES

- Keep your eye out for discounts attractively and unattractively offered
- Notice which ones appeal to you and why
- Model in your business the ones you like

I have a client right now who before we began working together asked me a series of questions to which the answers were all no. I was very uncomfortable and told her so. I am normally much more obliging than this I wanted her to know, but all of her overtures were for things I didn't want to give - a face-to-face meeting (no), a transfer of her fee to someone else should she decide to return to the day job (no) and something else I have forgotten (no). We are now in our third year of working together, and destined to be lifelong friends. Clients respect you for standing firm when that's appropriate. Equally, sometimes a client might ask for something I don't normally do and I'll go "Go on then!" but if they cross my boundaries once, that's enough for me to stand much firmer next time. Stand firm, me hearties. Stand firm.

Question 22

WHAT'S THE RIGHT PRICE FOR MY STUFF?

"You can't charge that, it's way too much!"

I love questions about how to charge for stuff and about pricing. It's so subjective, isn't it? Much room for squidginess lies herein. A rich seam for me.

I am an accountant and I know that even after having spent forty years with people and their money, I will NEVER understand how other people make their spending choices, or they mine.

Let us consider how much you would pay for:

- A meal out?
- A handbag?
- A haircut?
- A holiday?
- A car?
- A house?
- A new kitchen?

For every person who would pay what you would, based on some sort of inbuilt "ometer" about what something is worth to you, how much you can afford, and what is a "ridiculous" amount of money for something like that, there are gazillions of people living in entirely other financial realities, and multiples of those financial realities too.

My favourite example is the handbag because it is so easy to illustrate. You can buy a bag from Tesco, a bag for life, for 10p (controversially), what one of my colleagues, Carmel, used to call an "executive attaché case!" You can buy one to cart your stuff around in from Asda for say £5.99, probably less for all I know, I very rarely stray into Asda, I'm posh, me. Let's say you can buy one from Marks & Spencer for fifty quid. I don't know, I don't really go shopping. I have a bag that cost £650 and it was a gift. It is the only handbag I own and I shall use it every day for the rest of my life, out of respect for its beauty and craftsmanship but I would NEVER EVER have spent £650 of my own money on a handbag and probably never will, no matter how wealthy I am. But Posh Spice Victoria, Mrs Beckham, has all of those handbags like mine in all of the colours they make them in, and she does that each and every season.

Just look at all those different financial realities in just the handbag department! Amazing, isn't it?

That applies to everything you can think of. You have no idea what people will pay for a handbag, let alone for your lovely stuff or mine. If we think we do, we are making it up. The financial reality in which you and I live is probably different, as it is from everyone else we know.

My Ocado is your Tesco. You might insist on having your hair cut in Bond Street, where I favour someone who comes to the house and charges twenty quid. And my spending on my groceries but not on my hair, and you vice versa, is just the way people are. A formerly penniless bicycle-riding friend of my acquaintance, living on baked beans and pita bread when I first met her in the Nineties, had her hair cut in Chelsea in London by Nicky Clarke.

See how this works? People are bonkers when it comes to their spending choices. And as I was nearly going bankrupt in my first recession in the late Eighties and early Nineties, I was driving a BMW 5 series, and I bet people wondered about that. But you make your spending cuts on things you don't value in order to keep affording the things you do. And this is different with every single human being I've ever met. Shop at Asda so you can buy luxury clothes. Shop at Lidl while installing a hot tub in your garden. I could cite endless examples, truly.

When I was an accountant, clients used to allow me to believe they couldn't pay my bills. And while I was sitting in the back of an artisan cheese shop doing their accounts, I used to hear my clients' voices out front at the counter and know that they were paying through the nose for their delicious cheeses and expensive crisps in the shop. And whenever Marion and I, working together as a dynamic duo, used to cut our mutual client a fantabulous deal, because they led us to believe they were hard up, or we assumed they were, what did they do next? Nip off on a cruise with the dosh we'd just volunteered to save them, cutting off our noses to spite our faces! We laughed, oh yes. But we felt miserable too, stuck at home working for them on their websites and whatnot.

People find the money for what they want. My accounting clients would prioritise school fees, family holidays and Christmas before paying overdue invoices from me, and that meant we couldn't have those things until they did pay us. Augusts and Decembers were grim when it came to cash flow.

Often, in the bonkers, convoluted and complex world in which we live, people value stuff the more expensive the price tag. But it's good for us that they do, isn't it?

Try doubling your prices and see what happens. And if no-one notices, do it again!

- **What's the most you have ever paid for something?**
- **Did it take your breath away?**
- **How else did it make you feel?**
- **What meaning are you giving to that, if any?**
- **What assumptions have you made about what people will pay?**
- **What assumptions have you made about what to charge?**
- **Do they still hold good now that you've read my answer to Q22?**
- **What are you going to do about it?**

Question 23

HOW DO YOU GO FROM FREE TO FEE?

"How do you make a major change to your business, like charging where before it was free? What happens to the clients you already have?"

Good Q. I think you might want to consider charging NEW clients from hereon in and not necessarily making it universal. i.e. all old clients like it for free and don't like change, they got used to that and they are comfy with it. You don't need to charge them unless you want to. I might do that if I were cross with them for taking the Mickey but honestly, that's not a good abundant place from which to come at this. Don't punish your clients for your business decisions made in scarcer times.

We discuss this on the podcast quite often, and I discussed it with another client only this morning, it is a burning topic this summer. [Good job something's burning around here 'cos it ain't me! No, I lie. I am suntanned, just not quite enough for my liking.]

You know how if you are an early adopter of anything you can often get it free for life but newer customers pay? That business model is normal. I got in early with my online diary and it is free to me, forever I think. Newer adopters pay. All quite normal and businesslike and if people want freebies they can go elsewhere, or decide to stay and pay.

Could you align yourself with that sort of thinking?

I believe it is called being "grandfathered in" which means your clients keep the rate at which they joined and if that rate is free, then lucky those people. If you have people who are already enjoying your norm, whatever that may be, I probably wouldn't change that. Maybe they already form the useful solid base of your community, which makes your thing look like a lively attractive place so they do have a value to you. And now, new people wanting to join that same community will be invited to pay. And they will know no different and all will be well.

Don't throw the baby out with the bathwater, the answer to this question is no need to change your whole business model unless you want to. Just invite new clients from a certain date onwards to pay you. Job done! And you might consider, as we have already discussed in my Ask Judith Facebook Group, putting a Patreon or PayPal donate button on your website so that those who do get it for free can make a donation as often as they feel like it. Always make it easy for people to send you money.

http://OwnItThePodcast.com - are you listening yet?

We go live every Friday at 8 a.m. UK time. Subscribe via your fave podcast app (iTunes, Stitcher etc) and it automatically comes to you.

Question 24

WHAT'S THE BEST WAY TO ENFORCE MY TERMS?

"What do you do when you send your client an invoice at the end of month one, and another at the end of month two, and a third at the end of month three, by which point he hasn't paid any of them, and you haven't enforced your terms and you have no idea how to do that?"

Received wisdom is that you charge interest. Don't do that. If you can't collect your bill, which you can't so far, how on earth are you going to collect interest on top? Yes, there is legal provision for you to do that if you want to pursue your client through the UK small claims court on a point of principle and never work for them again, but who has time or energy for that? **Stop it immediately.**

Instead, this is teaching you the error of your ways.

You omitted a vital step when you took on this contract. You didn't have a discussion with your client in which you explained your terms (28 days) or that you are a much smaller business than his. And you didn't find out what the process is in his office for getting a bill paid. Does it go to him first for him to sign off? Then to accounts for processing? And only then to the MD who is the only one who can sign off on a payment run?

Dear God! Nightmare! All those people in the chain. So many places for it to go wrong and for them to lose your invoice. So many opportunities for them to dream up reasons why they haven't paid you. I wonder if you knew you were going to have to wait for three months to be paid, would you have taken on the work at all? Or would you have charged more, or what? It would have been a different proposition, right? I do hope your answer to that is yes. If not, see me after school.

My client wanted to know should she simply put 7 days on her fourth invoice and hope that would speed them up.

Nope. Firstly, they don't give a damn about your terms. They care about managing their own cash flow. Secondly, you didn't have the conversation. Thirdly, you didn't track your invoice through their organisation. You don't yet know the name of the bird in accounts who you can befriend, who understands your predicament and that you are a solopreneur who is about to start struggling to feed her kids (lay it on with a trowel) and you feel their treatment negates the value of all your hard work. Feelings. Feelings. Feelings. All in the absence of a good conversation.

So, what have we learned from this?

You might escalate your terms from 28 days to 7 days for all future clients, yes. But only if you have that conversation with your client at the beginning of every new relationship/project, the one about what your terms are, what their process is, what are the names and TELEPHONE NUMBERS of all the relevant personnel in the chain so that you can track your invoice through their system and do your bit to make sure they understand your terms since you are a new supplier.

Accounts departments don't notice or care about any of this. They pride themselves on hanging onto their own company's money for as long as possible, i.e. maximising their own cash flow. That's a win if you are an in-house accountant. Many businesses have been founded on precisely this practice and don't force me to name them here but I can come up with hundreds of them. Frankly I think it is amoral but, of course, we do not have to do business with them, that's entirely our choice.

OK, I realise you don't feel you have a choice to begin with. But you do. And you only want to do business with people who respect your terms. And even then you STILL need the phone number of the person responsible for getting your bill paid and you want them to be an ally. And you want to phone them to find out if your bill has landed on their desk yet, and what's the date of the next payment run in which yours will be included. And you make a note of all of this. Name. Number. Date. And if it doesn't happen precisely like that, you phone again. You don't email because they can ignore you and because it's cowardly. You need have no shame because you've done your work. They either do not have a good system for paying suppliers regularly and on time or their cash flow is dodgy and, if so, the sooner you know that the better before you decide to do work in months two and three.

Help them to help themselves. That ally in the accounts department is essential, as are your notes about when she said she'd pay you. If she didn't, she either forgot or her boss over-ruled her. So you need to call again and point it out (nicely-ish, coolly, assertively, unemotionally, certainly not either aggressively or defensively) and ask if she can confirm that you will be on the next run, and the date of that. A good relationship with Accounts will get you paid every time and prioritised over others who are too lazy or too nice to call and who choose instead to sit at home hoping.

Don't sit at home hoping. Be all over your own cash flow like a rash. When it comes right down to it, this is why we are employing ourselves for money. For the money! OK, I know there are other reasons but if you don't get paid too, the whole thing is loppy and disappointing and lots of other not so nice feelings which will spoil your whole enterprise. This absolutely does not need to turn into a battle, so there's no need to take up that energy. It's just business, all day long. It's about helping each other, specifically helping them to pay you within 7 days.

Elsewhere in this book clients and readers have expressed that asking for money is icky. In this instance it most certainly is not, because you have met your part of the contract, they are letting you down and failing by not doing theirs. I can talk you through how to handle this phone call. No biggie. Just because you'd be uncomfortable to be on the receiving end of such a call doesn't mean they are. It's their job, and it happens to them all day every day in their office. But you very definitely want to get yourself up their queue and the only way they can stop you phoning for your money is by paying you. Don't email, too passive. Phone!

But smoothing and easing the process to being paid all begins with that great conversation with your client within the business who is hiring you for money. You are not a monolith who can or will wait till kingdom come to get paid, your terms are 7 days and this is why. Can he make that work within his own system? If not, what's the best he can do? Is that good enough for you? Yes, OK good, we are in. No, and we'd be better off taking our talents elsewhere, because this doesn't meet our own needs.

I will tell you that I learned this from my days as an accountant. We used to issue clients with a bill at the end of the month or quarter or year, depending on the nature of our work for them. And wait, and wait, and wait to be paid. Grr. I hired a debt collector, a very nice woman called Jane who would come in one afternoon a week to phone clients and create a relationship with them and do what I have described above. Ask when they will pay. Note down the date. Phone to say thank you when it comes in, or to chivvy if it does not. Relationships, remember?

And, when I sold that business and started another, I selected businesses where this was all automated and mostly where nothing happens without FULL payment in advance. Which brings up another topic, stage payments if your contract is a big one or ongoing. But that's another topic for another day. But you can already see where I'd be headed with that one too, can't you? Always make it easy for your clients to pay.

NOTES

If you are uncomfortable talking about money, asking for money, thinking about money or feel you have a broken relationship with money, there is work to be done. Don't wait, although your employing yourself for money will cause you to change your mind about all of this in time, simply because it goes with the territory. If you have not already, start to accelerate your financial education and I will help and support you in this. Start with the Rich Dad Poor Dad books by Robert Kiyosaki and see where it leads you from there. If you can find a local game of Cashflow 101 and play it once a month for a year, you will discover the extent to which you are uncomfortable with money stuff and you can play firstly at fixing that. Then you can do it for real. Ask if you need support with this. Money isn't icky to me and soon it won't be to you either.

BREATHING SPACE – CHAPTER THREE - FINANCIAL

Chapter Three is all about money, in one way or another. Giving yourself away for free (no, just no), going from free to fee, pitching, discounting, enforcing your terms and charging what you are really worth or even whatever you like. The sky's the limit.

Which bits in here rumbled you? What did you realise or remember about the way you operate with money? How do you feel about those things now that you know you have choices?

What broken and loppy thoughts and feelings do you allow every day when it comes to money in your business and your life? How can you **stop it immediately?**

Who do you see who isn't like that? How would it feel to step into their shoes when it comes to matters of a financial nature, when it comes to negotiating your price and determining your value?

How do you pay for things; easily and abundantly, or from a place of skint and scarce? Is that a good vibrational match for how you want it to be with your clients and customers?

What do you love to buy, whatever its price? What do you always find the money for? Imagine your clients and customers doing that. They will, you know.

Take a breather and think through how it feels to be employing yourself, particularly from the money perspective. How would you love it to be different from the way it is today?

How close to that are you and what's going to help you bridge that gap?

Maybe you are one of those who has this money stuff cracked? No, not yet? But nearly? Good on you. This was my issue too. We teach what we most need to learn, remember.

Use this space to write down some helpful observations about money and bring them to me to talk about and let's get all the baddies routed and bring in your lovely abundant new way of being.

CHAPTER FOUR

Marketing

Question 25

WILL I EVER LEARN TO LOVE MARKETING AND SELLING?

Gentle Reader, prepare yourself. I think this might be the one you most need to read but least want to. Nothing sells itself. Which means you **do** have to learn both marketing and sales, yes. And, in my considerable experience, almost no-one wants to do that. It brings out more bonkersness than almost any other type of question in my work.

Marketing accounts for about fifty percent of the work I do. If I didn't market myself, no-one would ever find me or become a client. And they don't just need to discover I exist to become a client. They need to hear about me. Keep an eye on me. Decide when the time is right for them to make an investment in themselves and their business, and be ready to get their credit card out. That process can be a long time; sometimes it takes many years. A client I took on in 2015 said she'd heard about me in 2010 and I remember thinking "What took you so long?" which is funny, but it is also very much the point. Every time I am on the receiving end of a comment like this I share it with my coaching groups, Club 100 and Small Business Big Magic, to prepare them for how long clients can be in your marketing pipeline before they spend money with you. Think back, what's the longest it has ever taken you to buy something? That!

Marketing is time-consuming and sales are not. Once a client is ready to do business, that's breathtakingly fast, as fast as it takes for someone to send you some digital cash. In a heartbeat or two hours, as fast as your own bank permits.

If, for instance, you had gone to market in 2010 and known you had to wait until 2015 for this client to get her purse out, would you have waited, would you have carried on marketing, or would you have given up and gone back to the day job?

Not everyone takes so long. Sometimes a potential new client will Google me, find my website, make up his mind he likes the cut of my jib, and send me (a complete stranger) some money today before we've even spoken. All sorts exist in the world, and everywhere in between those two extremes. But the point is that if you expect to be overwhelmed with business when you first take your thing to market, well **stop it immediately**. That's not how it is, mostly. Although please also prepare for magic and miracles, my stock in trade.

When I was an accountant I didn't have to do marketing so it all came as a bit of a shock to me too when I began life as a coach.

In the accounting years, I remember once in the Eighties paying for some adverts in a glossy local magazine which was delivered free door-to-door. I am sure you remember the sort of thing. That doesn't really happen anymore, although a swift Google reveals that Southside Magazine, to which I refer, and which then went on to become S.W. Magazine, looks like it may have been replaced by something called The Resident. Anyway, you get the gist. You've probably got your own local equivalent?

After about six months, when I had spent about a thousand pounds in advertising, I remember calculating my ROI (return on investment). How much had a thousand pounds in advertising brought me in business? I can't remember the precise figure but I do remember it was at least ten times that, maybe more. And so we kept on doing it. Forever. Not, I think, in the end, that the advert used to bring us lots of clients. Word of mouth did that, but when a referral was made the new client had always heard of us thanks to the magazine advertising.

So when I became a coach, advertising was all I knew. So I had a go at advertising my coaching business. I can tell you now, that doesn't work. I took some of my own advice and **stopped it immediately**.

I notice how little attention I pay to adverts these days. I have an Ad Blocker on my computer so I don't see them and I don't have a TV so I don't see them there either. You Gov occasionally ask me about how many adverts I have seen for this, that and the other and the answer is always none because, of course, I have taken deliberate steps to make sure I don't see them. There are exceptions. I am an avid user of Amazon and they are pretty good at telling me that if I like this, then I'll probably like that too and I am as susceptible to those promotions as anyone else.

However, back to my point. If people are choosing, like me, not to see ads anymore, then how are your potential buyers going to find out about you? There's an exception to that rule, obviously, and I'll come back to it.

When new clients come and tell me about their dreams for their business and/or income generation, I always have an eye out for the marketing thereof, because I know all too well that unless they relish that, there is very little point in their going to all the trouble to set themselves up if they don't have a route to sales.

I have played in my various businesses with all sorts of marketing; adverts, as I've said, and direct mail where a pretty postcard comes through your real-world letterbox and either you need that service now or you pin the postcard up on your kitchen cork board until the day comes when you do.

If I am looking for something today, I ask Google or Facebook. Youngsters apparently use YouTube as their search engine. How do you find out about what you are looking for? What's your route to buying a product or service? How could you turn that around and use it to bring clients and customers to you? That's the game here.

And what if you are not prepared to do that?

Honestly? If you are not prepared to learn to love marketing and sales, don't bother. That's the bad news.

The good news is that I am 100% confident and humdingeringly certain that I can help you find a route to market that might initially terrify you but which, in due course, you will come to love. Because unless you come to love it, you won't keep doing it and you will always need to keep doing it to protect your business from the syndrome known as feast and famine, which means you market your business, you get paying clients, so you stop marketing. Then when you've fulfilled those orders or contracts, you are back to zero again. Nope. Marketing has to happen forever. FOREVER. Just look around you. Every little product you buy is advertised by its producer forever, even a Kit Kat. Who thought we'd need reminding to buy one (or a few) of those? But we do.

And this is where we might (MIGHT, I say) have a look at your profile, specifically whether or not you are an introvert or an extrovert.

In short, an extrovert might leave the house to find business. So that's networking, public speaking, and developing a profile where you are highly visible to all. Typically, these people in Wealth Dynamics* parlance would be Stars* and Supporters* and people who are "all down the right-hand side" as I call them. And, quirkily, Mechanics* who are technically more introvert than me (50/50) but seem to crave being with people too. Good. Go and find your people, hang out with them and let them know who you are and what you do that way. I'd rather die, frankly. And networking is very much a LONG game. In fact, I have clients who've done networking for years and never had a worthwhile client from it, but I tell you what they do get. They get their social needs met. They get out of the house and they meet people and that cheers them up a bit. There are exceptions, of course. But have a look at who you know who's making gazillions from networking and ask yourself are you prepared to be like them, even a little bit? If so, good! You have your route to market. If no, then we are still on the lookout for yours. It's there, trust me. It's there.

Us introverts (or 50/50s) do it all online. All done from home. Alone.

And if that doesn't excite you, then ignore this next bit. Social media is whatever you believe it to be. Good. Bad. Meh. But it does enable me to reach potential clients the world over, using my favourite ways of communicating with them via the written and the spoken word. The written word stuff includes my website, blogging, enticing people to read my newsletter, sharing that online for those that won't opt in, and creating wonderful ways to connect with people via Facebook mainly. The spoken word way is a weekly podcast where, this week, we will record show #150, another long game. I love all of these routes to market. If I didn't, I wouldn't do them. That's absolutely key. What do you love, even if it starts out as what are you prepared to experiment with?

People are in two minds about social media, and which platforms they prefer depending on their inclinations towards how something looks or reads or sounds. And if we go back to my favourite idea of Sell As You Buy, then how do you like to consume content on social media? Create your own marketing on that same platform and draw to you people who love it in the way that you do.

As it happens I love Facebook, but it wasn't always so. I came off Facebook once as I thought it was for the kids. And then I went back on and all the kids moved off (those two weren't exactly cause and effect in the way that reads!). And FB now enables me to connect with people, chat to them, engage with them, share with them, enlighten and inform them and receive all those things in return. And, for me, they are ALL a form of marketing, either incredibly subtle or bang-right-in-your-face when I use it to ask for the business directly and deliberately. And mostly it is somewhere in between. Facebook has become my main route to market. It is a place where I can share myself with my potential future clients and where they can get to know me, to like me and to trust me. And I do it all for free. Though I don't rule out using FB Ads to sell this book, I don't think that FB Ads are my route to market to sell my coaching and mentoring services, but never say never. The organic Facebook game I play achieves the same desired end results.

One of my friends used to like to pop into my office in the olden days and weigh the post and stick the stamps on and take the letters round to the post office. She called it playing Post Offices. If you cannot find a way to make marketing and sales a game that appeals as much to you as that did to my friend, I fear you are on a hiding to nothing.

As an example, when a writer comes to me with plans to self-publish, I let her know that my view is that writing the book is the (relatively) easy bit. As it has been with this one. I think I can probably get this book written and published within three months, but my marketing plan to do it full justice will be for three years, and that includes updating the book annually so each summer I will repeat what I am currently putting myself through, but it will give me enough marketing material each time I do it for multiple uses of the same content, without taking anything away from the book itself which will be a completely different experience. As it happens, I am loving it even more than I anticipated, and that's the surprise and delight with marketing, as you too will discover, I promise.

It **will** be the same with your business. Perhaps you could already deliver your service or sell your product today, this very afternoon, but unless you are telling the world about it or blowing your own trumpet as you probably call it too, then you simply aren't going to have enough customers.

I think this reason alone is sufficient to hire a business coach and mentor. Because if you don't like it, you aren't going to do it. You are going to close your mind to lots of lovely different routes to your market, you won't even notice ones you don't think about or know exist. You'll do yourself and your future customers a terrible disservice by keeping yourself a secret when you could be helping people and employing yourself for money. And all your exciting ideas will wither and die.

What a tragedy that would be!

And sales, Judith? What about sales? Ah well… get your marketing right and sales are easy.

- Who do you see that markets in a way that is attractive to you, whether or not you have bought from them yet or ever?
- And vice versa. What do you observe that offends you?
- Which ones will you model, or will you invent your own way?
- How will you adapt marketing to suit your own business and your own personality, ethics and values?

Keep your eyes peeled all the time and start noticing lovely marketing. Borrow the best bits until you feel confident to invent your own genius iterations.

Question 26

WHY DO I FEEL LIKE I AM BEING UNPROFESSIONAL IN GIVING AWAY ALL MY BEST WORK?

Together with my clients and colleagues and friends a few of us have been reading THANK & Grow Rich by Pam Grout this summer. I put the word THANK in caps every time I use it because many people misread it and think I am recommending Think & Grow Rich which is a fine book too, but not the one we are reading together during August 2017.

Grouty was looking over my shoulder as I was writing this, my own book.

Quite early on in her book Pam says something which puts me in mind of the perpetual challenge experienced by a client who always tells me that everything on social media is a waste of time, including blogging. She's a professional writer and if she's not being paid to write then she's not a pro, she's diminishing her craft and she's giving it all away for free.

I half agree with her, the other half of me believes in giving away your best stuff, that's the way **my** world works but it isn't my client's reality. I certainly take her point. However, I also believe it goes to scarcity.

Pam Grout's middle name is Abundance.

Pam says:

"***It's not fair*** *and other patterns of thinking that lead us around by the nose. Anytime we look at a situation and feel that it should be other than it is, the malevolent puppeteer in our brain erects a wall of static.*

Here are a few other plot points the evil puppeteer uses to heckle us:

- *Something needs to be fixed*
- *There's only so much to go around*
- *If I give of myself, people will take advantage*
- *If I follow my heart, I'll be alone*
- *If I pursue my passion, I'll be a laughing stock*
- *It is dangerous to follow my joy"*

A couple of those made an appearance in this book, even before I read Pam's list, but you'll notice the pertinent one is right there, slap bang in the middle: "If I give of myself, people will take advantage."

My client is rare. She is a woman very much in a man's world and her experience of being taken advantage of in those circumstances is true for her to the extent that it has become a fact. I have listened to her as she's told me her stories. I would occasionally try to winkle in a thought that if she could change her mind the results would change too, but these beliefs were far too embedded to change overnight or possibly at all. To my client they are facts. I am not so wedded to my version of the world that it is essential to convert all my clients to my way or the highway. So we agreed to respectfully disagree with one another, but we always gave each other a fair and equal hearing, out of mutual respect.

Oddly, no sooner had she stopped being a formal client and moved to PWYW, than I noted her sharing a lot more of her content online in a way I would have wished she'd done when she was with me. I commented immediately upon how much I was enjoying her social media output and she replied that she had found an easy way to do it.

I wonder what miracles and opportunities will come from her new-found ease with free and fantastic top-notch content? And, of course, her content is top-notch, she's a pro, remember?

NOTES

- **What do you give away for free?**
- **How do you feel about that?**
- **Are you happy with those feelings, or is there a useful change of heart or mind in the offing?**

Question 27

WHY IS IT TAKING ME SO LONG TO GET MY WEBSITE LIVE?

This is one of those questions I wanted to answer with "I have no earthly idea!" Only I do.

Provided you decide to go with a self-hosted WordPress website, and with other solutions for all I know, every single word on your website can be changed in a heartbeat.

So, don't get hung up on your website.

Many people don't visit them or even bother to read them anymore anyway.

Even those that do visit do not chronologically read every word in the order you intend.

Keep the copy on your website very short, above the fold, don't make us scroll, the 2017 visitor doesn't have an attention span, they'll click away faster than you can possibly imagine. Do not dwell on finding the perfect word. Go live as soon as possible and let's crack on, knowing you can change every word in a nanosecond if you want. And every day if it comes to that, and more often still though I don't recommend it. Then you'd be finding busy work for yourself.

No-one appreciates a perfect website, not a potential buying customer anyway.

You don't even need a website to get a client. So stop fussing!

The number of clients coming to me who have never even visited my website increases daily. They come to me directly from Facebook itself which is just the entire world in one easy accessible mostly free marketplace. Much easier to go to them there perhaps, than get them to come to you which is a complex, expensive and time-consuming process anyway and possibly one which is about to be superseded.

If I were starting again today to market myself I wouldn't bother with a website. I'd have a Facebook Business Page hooked up to my MailChimp list server. And all the thousands of pounds I've put into websites could go into Facebook Ads instead.

My website is long overdue an overhaul. There are several reasons for this. Of the two people I might have chosen to work with on this, one died and the other got out of doing websites, and who can blame her?

But even though I am aware the current iteration is due an overhaul, recently a new paying client said to me:

"If you don't mind me saying, what set you apart and attracted me was that your site wasn't really corporate and I could feel a real person behind it."

Mind.

MIND?

I could have kissed him!

But you get the point, don't you? This is all SO subjective. One woman's overdue overhaul is another man's perfection. Well, not perfection exactly or even close, but good enough for him to want to consider becoming a client, opt into my newsletter list, listen to our podcast, sign up for an exploratory call, decide to start working with me and send me some money online pronto.

Good enough. Good enough. Good enough, that's all a website (or anything in small business) needs to be. Perfection is for the birds. Expensive birds with fat wallets. Know any of those gagging to work with you? No, me neither.

Only you can work out what you want to be found for and known for via your website. The antidote to corporate is absolutely me so my website is doing that job for me rather well it seems, which is just peachy.

The overhaul can wait. It's ego anyway.

Don't get hung up on this. Start making money today, via Facebook like me, or any route. You could just ask someone at the bus stop to become your client, and you wouldn't be the first! Let's discuss those other routes too. And if you really feel you still need a website, you can bring that on at the same time, as well as not instead of. You don't need all your ducks in a row before you can start to tell the world who you are, what you do and how you can help. Or before you start to ask for the business. You just feel like you do.

Feelings, again. Those little devils.

NOTES

- Are you fussing about your website?
- Why?
- What are you really putting off?
- What (or who) are you hiding from?
- Where could you more effectively put your time and effort and money?
- How can you make your first sale before your website even goes online?

Question 28

HOW CAN I BE LOUD ENOUGH OR DIFFERENT ENOUGH TO GET NOTICED?

Two clients generously donated to this topic.

The first client said that she has a feeling that her voice isn't loud enough to be heard, even if her idea is good and valid.

And the second client said there is so much noise and so much marketing going on everywhere you look that she can't possibly cut through that, no matter how good she is at what she does because no-one's listening so why bother with an exercise in futility?

Although these might look the same, I sense a lack of confidence in the first and a fatigue with the way other people do marketing in the second.

Loud first. Do we need to be loud? I don't think so. I think we need to be on fire with what we have to offer the world, so excited about our thing that we can't help but share it. I think we have to feel that it is fit for purpose, that it helps people and that we will get better at it as we do it with real live customers and clients. And then we have to be visible. And visibility doesn't necessarily mean shouting from the rooftops or using a bullhorn. But it does mean finding your route to market which you enjoy and employ every day, not in fits and starts.

My own example is a good one so I keep using it in this book:

1. *Do you know how many business coaches there are in the world?* **More than we can count.**

2. *Do I feel I have been as loud as the most successful of them?* **No.**

3. *Do I feel I have been visible enough for the right clients to find me and for us to do good work together?* **Yes.**

4. *Did this happen overnight?* **No, it did not. I have been marketing myself for fifteen years and enjoying it and doing it every day.**

What have I experimented with that I didn't like so that I stopped it immediately? Face to face networking. Yuk! Not for me, never was, never will be. Does that mean I am not a networker? No. I have collected many useful people in Judith-world through my work both as an accountant and as a coach, forty years' worth of contacts, people who do a million different things. And nothing brings me greater pleasure than connecting those people in ways that I hope will be useful for both parties. For instance, I refer clients to all sorts of resources other than myself if I think that will be more useful than our work together or if it will supplement it. But formal networking at breakfast, lunch, tea or dinner? *Non merci!*

I don't leave the house to network, and yet something came upon me during August to invite a contact round to spend the afternoon with me in the garden. Most unlike me and yet, once the invitation was issued on a whim, I followed through and we both thoroughly enjoyed ourselves, so many ways to skin a cat with the networking thing without my even leaving home. I pride myself on being good at it online too, remembering most people I've ever had dealings with and some I only know from having met them online, many of whom have never even been clients but I know what they do and they know what I do and we help each other by referral. It's just who I am. Is that loud? No. Is it helpful? Yes.

I bet you do things like this too. And you think perhaps they are quiet, but they add up. No need to be loud unless you want to be.

When it comes to cutting through all the other marketing out there, and resisting it, and not liking it, and not wanting to be like it, you don't have to be or do anything you see others be and do which makes you feel uncomfortable. If anything, this is what I love most about marketing.

I always say to anyone who asks that I use Facebook 100% for marketing and yet it looks a lot of the time like I am just having fun. And indeed I am. But that is also marketing for me, doing double-duty, helping me to be visible and to connect with strangers who eventually turn up in my diary.

We are back in received wisdom territory again. I am reading a book right now by an expert in her field and there's plenty of received wisdom in it. Some of that I reject, and some I already know but am happy to be reminded about. And I notice as I read through that I am mentally ticking off - yes, no, maybe. Yes means I already know how to do that, I like doing that and I will do more of it. No means not in a month of Sundays. And maybe means ooh, I'd forgotten about that or never considered it and maybe I would experiment with that and see how it goes or it means ooh, good idea, didn't think of that one, can't wait to have a go.

But I am weighing all the received wisdom in the book against my own innate wisdom. OK, I'll grant you this is born of being pretty confident in my own abilities and filters after all these years, but marketing in 2017 also requires me to learn new things which are stretchy in the learning but satisfying and fun and useful. I learned something new over the weekend which was time-consuming and hard. I can't tell you how many times during the video training (remember how much I HATE video?) I contemplated switching off, hiring someone to do it for me, or simply listening without focus while multitasking with Facebook. But I didn't. Because in this particular example I knew it was something I wanted to learn and which would help me "cut through" as my pal says.

TBH, I don't think much about cutting through. As I have already written in this book, I don't really believe in comparisons. My first client here is an artist and my second is a website designer, and although I've known plenty of those in my time, neither of these two women do what they do in a way that is in the least like anyone else. Our unique set of skills and talents and, more importantly, our human being through which they are delivered is perfect for our ideal clients. We don't need to be loud, we just need to be ourselves. And we choose to believe that we can make a difference to each of our clients by showing up and offering them our best work.

If that's the message you communicate through all that you do, whether marketing message or client service/delivery, you will be absolutely fine and you can drop all marketing-related antipathy and bonkersness in time, as you prove the opposite of both of these assumptions. It might not happen overnight. But do not rule out that possibility. Magic and miracles are our stock in trade, remember?

- **If not loud or different, what words would you use to describe your own marketing?**
- **What would be even better than that?**
- **What one thing could you do now to get that shiny new ball rolling?**

Question 29

MUST I BLOW MY OWN TRUMPET?

Blowing your own trumpet is what my clients call it when they feel uncomfortable about what they perceive they have to do by way of marketing, i.e. talk about themselves in a show-offy way about how wonderful they are, their business is and the results their products and services help their clients achieve.

It is just another example of where we are all a bit naturally ALL or NOTHING. Our first assumption, before we have examined anything, always appears to be A or Z, black or white. We forget about the almost infinite number of choices and gradations there are between the two extremes of anything.

If you are quite a shy person, you naturally assume you are going to have to stand on a very tall box with a bullhorn at Hyde Park Corner to blow your own trumpet in a useful marketing sense. You are not.

Here are my tips.

1. Keep an eye out for marketing done subtly and well and in a way that is your taste. Keep an eye out also for it being done outrageously and in-yer-face, admire both and know you don't have to do either for you will be finding your own unique way that feels great and which it just so happens your clients and customers also appreciate. Your marketing will be what we call a brand match for your ideal customer. Whoa, Judith! You went a bit jargony there. Yes, I did. Apologies, Gentle Soul.

2. Model it, and borrow the best bits. Be prepared to experiment. Come out slowly, or as fast as all hell. You won't know how it's working until you have a go. Let's crack on then, but at your own speed. I will probably encourage you to do it a bit faster than you'd like. You want to eat, don't you?

3. The funny thing about this is how quickly we acclimatise. Your next problem after you find peace with your trumpet work is that you will be asking me for ways to accelerate and amplify it. Ha! Gotcha.

4. Be an engager, not a broadcaster. What's the difference? A broadcaster makes an announcement and disappears, not noticing or caring if we have replied or responded. And days later, if at all, they pop back and they might make a cursory response to ours on theirs. YUK. I really dislike that and try as hard as possible not to be a broadcaster. I'll start a conversation and intend to respond to everyone who contributes to it or engages with it, except perhaps the nutters and sometimes I even embrace them too. But that's entirely my choice.

5. Establish rapport. This is a very fine art and one which I am not sure you can learn, but perhaps you can. Anyone I see failing at this, and they are mostly conspicuous by their absence, have not yet found a way to connect with their audience. Keep looking. I'll help. I love marketing, me.

6. Know that you are not, in a marketing sense, 100% unique. Whatever it is that you like and share, however weird, will find a sizeable audience that likes it too. As I am writing this chapter of my book I am staying as a guest in a house that overlooks a piece of land where over the three-day weekend at the end of August they are doing battle re-enactments. There's the rat-a-tat-tat of gunfire. Each to their own. But the fact is that's a tribe of people bound together by a common interest which I might think bizarre but I bet you know or have met or have heard of someone who likes that. So it will be with whatever your quirky interests are. Flaunt your quirks and give people who share your weirdness a chance to connect with you that way. That's rapport. Easy, yes?

7. Be good at one social media channel, not across all of them. It's probably enough, unless what you do is social media marketing for yourself and

your clients and, in that case, go bonkers and fill your boots. One platform done well is enough for a one-man or one-woman band. I ignore all of them now except Facebook. I used to have a go at all of them, except the visual ones, nothing there for me. I've even had the courage of my convictions and come off LinkedIn after it failed to produce a client after 15 years. Doh. I could have packed that one in ages ago then, get my point?

8. If at the end of all of this you still feel you are blowing your own trumpet, you are doing it all wrong. See me after school.

Put down that trumpet, get off the box and tell me how you are going to share your fire with those you can help.

Question 30

HOW DO I GET COMFY WITH SELF-PROMOTION?

"Is one of the difficulties entrepreneurs face talking about themselves? When you work for an organisation you can hide behind corporate messaging, but when you are your business then any publicity is ultimately about you, and that is a lot less comfortable."

Thanks again to one of those in the Roll of Honour for bringing yet another great question.

I don't feel this. And lots of my clients don't either. Did I once, way back? Probably yes. My memory is a bit dim on this one, but I know I would be more in the reluctant camp generally speaking. Nerves about this when you start out are normal, good and healthy.

Loads of people do feel discomfort, especially at the beginning.

Here's how I think of it.

Obviously, show-offs and certain Starry* personality types love this from the get-go; being the centre of attention, talking about themselves, and having the spotlight on them. Let's assume they don't need our help today.

For the rest of us, there are lots of ways to find comfort in being in the spotlight, or at least in that sort of spotlight, the one where you are interviewed, the one where you talk about yourself and your projects and your business, having first taken care to showcase your expertise and offer something of value to your listener or reader or watcher.

Any tips I would give a client are as follows, in no particular order of importance.

Practice makes perfect. You will get better and more comfortable with this in time. No-one is good at anything from Day One, and we cannot wait until we are excellent because we cannot get to that place of comfort without first having a few plucky goes. I think both the interviewer and the listener are sympathetic to newbie nervousness because it is only natural, and vulnerability is often very attractive where overconfidence is not. I already know you are good enough for this and in your heart of hearts, so do you.

Until then, remember that you don't have to tell anyone anything you don't want them to know. You don't have to get naked, figuratively speaking, unless you want to. So work out what you want to reveal, if anything, and what not. If a question makes you feel uncomfortable, don't answer it. Do what the politicians do and answer the question you wish they'd asked instead. Interviewers are used to that and will respond accordingly, or not even notice. Only Jeremy Paxman will bring you back and grill you, over and over, until you do. But he's not interviewing you, is he? They are not all Rottweilers, thankfully.

Mostly an interviewer will send questions in advance. If they offer that, accept it. If they don't, ask if they can/will. Obviously, this doesn't necessarily happen if the interview is happening at very short notice because it is topical today, or newsworthy immediately. But that probably doesn't happen with our business, or not until we announce to the media that we are up for that. I am not. I cannot and will not dump my clients for the convenience of the media. I know lots of people who do. The choice is always ours, as with anything. Just because people ask, it doesn't mean we have to accept though you did, I know, for the good of your volunteer project. Brave! Good on you.

You can always ask what the interviewer intends to cover. Be prepared. Dib. Dib. Dib.

There's no such thing as bad publicity. I know this is a cliché, but what I observe is that this is truer today than it has ever been. Let me explain. I've watched TV programmes about business people that I thought made them look absolutely loathsome. But others noticed only that they were famous because they were on the telly, and these days (sorry) being famous because you are on the telly = A Good Thing in our world (not to me it isn't, by the way), and it is almost irrelevant what you said or how you behaved or how you came across. And since you are not loathsome, you will do better than those publicity-hungry types I felt so antipathetic towards. We don't all like or dislike the same qualities in another human being; that's worth remembering.

Some people will see or hear you and connect with you. Others won't. And they won't notice or care and you won't make any dent on their awareness, so again you can't get it wrong because those in the first camp will become aware of you in only a good way.

Preparation is key. You know this already because you are a pro. Even if you don't use the vast majority of your prep, no matter. Being well prepared makes you feel more confident in the moment.

My own personal choice is not to accept invitations to be on TV or any visual medium. But I am always happy to give interviews in the written and spoken word or face to face, and I am often amazed when I listen to myself later, as I pretty much always do, sometimes more than once, to hear my own wisdom coming through. I promise you I think "Who is that brilliant woman?" and then I realise it's me. I think this will be exactly what you are surprised and delighted to discover about yourself. Once you become more aware of your own expertise, this just becomes easier and easier to share.

Only accept invitations from your favourite types of media, where comfort is more likely.

Talk about your work, rather than yourself, always remembering that people are fascinated by your human story too so any interviewer worth their salt is likely to want to draw you on that at least a little, or perhaps as a warm-up to the meat of the discussion.

Most of my clients who go through this process report back afterwards that they loved it, they got a buzz from it, they felt "high" when it ended (adrenaline), it was surprisingly easy, they got good feedback from it, they got good publicity from it and, ultimately, they got clients from it. Keep your eyes on the prize.

If in doubt, don't. Find another way to get publicity for your business which you do relish. Press releases perhaps? What else I wonder? Let's get our heads together on that.

Today's media sound bites are wrapping tomorrow's chips. Sorry to mix my metaphors but I know you know what I mean. There's so much media noise in the world, almost no-one will notice. Sorry, but it's true. And once you HAVE cracked this, you'll be asking me how you can get more and better publicity. Trust me, I know that's true. It happens all the time, and the transition from terrified reluctant newbie to would-be media tart is often astonishingly fast.

It'll be over in the blink of an eye and you'll wish it had lasted longer. Ha!

Always listen to it back so you can improve, if there's room for any. Then forget it. It's gone out on the airwaves now, it's gone, there's nothing you can do about it now. See if you can get a link to the recording for use in your own publicity materials, but only if it's any good! Sometimes you will be allowed to use the media logo on your website - as featured on the BBC or in Marie Claire, or whatever. That can be useful cred.

Always ask that they link to your website or wherever the listener can find out more about you/whatever you are promoting. The media who often think you will do this because they ask and without payment, for the honour of it (LOL) and are notoriously slack about this. Agree it in advance. Pull them up on it if they fail. They really need to get better at this, you aren't doing it for the good of your health, it's a two-way deal. You help them get content for their show, they help you get publicity for your biz.

Remember to ask yourself "what's in it for me?" If there's nothing in it for you, just say no. This last tip is discretionary.

Visualisation might help you. "See" yourself on stage/TV being brilliant. Ditto EFT and/or NLP and/or hypnosis, any of which can help you to see yourself stepping into the shoes of someone who you admire precisely because they are as confident as you would like to be in interview situations, talking about themselves and their work. There's always someone to model who has an admirable way of doing whatever you want to be doing effortlessly and elegantly too.

Question 31

HOW DO I ASK FOR THE BUSINESS?

When clients tell me it's not working and they are in financial extremis I often say "have you asked for the business?"

This means that we should stop being so subtle with our marketing now and again and ask for what we want.

On social media, that means not just sharing great content but reminding the consumers of said content why we are doing that. And asking for what we want.

What you want might be for people to share your great content. I find that if you ask them to do that, they will. Don't be frightened or forget to ask them to do that. PLS SHARE. Or PLS RT.

But every now and again, depending on how much and what type of content you are putting out as part of your marketing, you must remind consumers that you are not doing this for the good of your health.

I blog, and write a weekly newsletter and co-create a weekly podcast, and spend about 50% of my working week creating and sharing great content, and curating the content of others which is on point for my fans and followers, clients and potential clients, and whilst I love to do that, I don't do it for the craic. I do it so that some of the consumers will eventually become clients, or at least that they will know about me and recommend me to others when those people are looking for a business coach.

And I am unapologetic about this. And you will learn to be completely comfortable with this too.

So at the end of the podcast and in the newsletters and blog posts and on social media, I remind people where they can find out more about working with me. If I forget to do that, am I wasting my time with my marketing? Yes, probably. Even though I am having a lovely time.

If you have a newsletter list, one of the ways of asking for the business is to write to your readers that you are making them an offer right now. And it may be a bargain, or not. And it may be time sensitive, or not. It doesn't have to be either of those things. But it has to be useful and it has to be what they want and it has to meet your own needs too. If you don't have a newsletter list yet, you can do some gorgeous adverts (paid or unpaid) on Facebook using pretty memes and tempting copy.

No-one will buy anything from you if you don't make them an offer, if you don't ask for the business.

It is usually the one bit we have overlooked. We've been too subtle in the marketing, or we haven't reminded them what we are selling, or we haven't tempted them with something lovely to buy this week or month.

People love to buy. There's no shame in offering them your stuff. They can't buy it if they don't know about it and, just like a plate of tempting homemade biscuits, who can resist one if offered elegantly and without any attachment to whether or not someone takes you up on your offer? Great if they do, great if they don't, no scarcity round these parts.

By the way, whilst writing, who do you know who would love this book? Would you tell them about it, please? Or send them a copy as a prezzie? Thank you.

- **Have you been too subtle?**
- **Have you made your potential clients an offer?**
- **How will you experiment with asking for the business and being just a little bit more cheeky?**

BREATHING SPACE – CHAPTER FOUR - MARKETING

Chapter Four is all about busting the bonkersness around marketing, specifically giving it all away, selling it, websites, being loud enough, being visible, being found, blowing your own trumpet, getting comfy with self-promotion and asking for the business.

On a scale of 1-10, how comfy do you feel with all of that now?

Is there work still to be done to make life feel just easier?

When do you feel inspired to start? No, come on, you must feel a little tickle of interest about one aspect of marketing, surely?

Do you know if you are an introvert or extrovert? Do you want to do your marketing face-to-face, or online?

Have you had paying clients and customers already? If so, how did you get them? What's working? Do more of that! And if you don't know what's working, shame on you. See me in my study - NOW!

Come on, we can do this. We can make this fun and easy. You will love it. Or starve. Which do you foresee in your own future? Clue: I have only met a tiny number of clients who have given up and gone back to the day job 'cos they couldn't crack this. I am confident you will find a way to learn to love marketing too.

So, take this breathing space to work out and brainstorm your favourite routes to your first client and your first sale. And if you don't know what they are yet, where do you fancy having a go? How will you get your first paying customer/make your first sale? That is absolutely life-changing and thrilling and a moment you will never forget. And once you get past that point, you are off. This thing's only gonna work!

Here's the space for your thinking and notes. You know how this works now. Let me know if you are stuck. I have an inkling you won't be. We can all do this. If in doubt, go back to the fire. What are you on fire with? What's your mission? What's the thing that never goes away? What would be your favourite way to tell the world all about it? Go!

CHAPTER FIVE

Personal

Question 32

WHO AM I TO...?

You are a unique and wonderful human being. I know this because I know you personally, I have been your coach, and you and your lovely husband have been to visit me in my home.

Listen very carefully, I shall say this only once.

If you don't live your life to the fullest, no-one will give a damn except you, and those that love and respect you like your husband, those beautiful children (once they are old enough), your wonderful friends, and me.

It is your job (and yours alone) to live your own unique life in whatever way that lights your candle, that might be by business achievement/employing yourself for money, or not.

But your light doesn't dim anyone else's. *Au contraire,* Beloved.

Implicit in your question is what will other people think of me.

Who cares? I honestly couldn't give a hot damn, and neither should you and I almost never tell anyone to should. Can't bear shoulds, me, but I feel a bit shouldy about this one.

Get on and do whatever you want to do anyway, and let people think whatever they are going to think, which is mostly a lot less than you hallucinate because they are all far too self-obsessed and crippled with the same anxieties.

I am sure you know the very famous quote by Marianne Williamson from her book A Return to Love. I am going to quote it anyway (below) and tell you that when someone first faxed it into my office in the Nineties, I cried. That's how much it spoke to me. That's how much I was still connected to the part of me and the time in my life in which I was under-achieving by my own standards, no-one else's.

Your playing small serves no-one, most especially not you or those gorgeous shiny children of yours. Put this completely misapplied modesty aside and let's crack on. You are powerful beyond measure. Let us both get on with the business of liberating others if that's the (accidental) result of living by our own light.

"Our deepest fear is not that we are inadequate. Our deepest fear is that we are powerful beyond measure. It is our light, not our darkness that most frightens us. We ask ourselves, 'Who am I to be brilliant, gorgeous, talented, fabulous?' Actually, who are you not to be? You are a child of God. Your playing small does not serve the world. There is nothing enlightened about shrinking so that other people won't feel insecure around you. We are all meant to shine, as children do. We were born to make manifest the glory of God that is within us. It's not just in some of us; it's in everyone. And as we let our own light shine, we unconsciously give other people permission to do the same. As we are liberated from our own fear, our presence automatically liberates others."

- Marianne Williamson - A Return to Love: Reflections on the Principles of "A Course in Miracles"

NOTES

Do you know this gorgeous song by Brian Kennedy - Get on With Your Short Life? I share it because it came to mind when I was writing to you. https://www.youtube.com/watch?v=5NClpvIzcUI And what a hunk, eh? You can thank me later for that.

Question 33

WHY IS THERE NO MONEY IN MY IDEAS YET?

One of the few types of client I have found it most difficult to help to employ themselves for money is the one who's in love with ideas. She's a Scanner, so she tells me. Oh God, I think. Another one. Yes, I've read that book too and it is wonderful, but it gives us permission to be scattered. No, it gives us permission to glory in being scattered.

Newsflash! At our level, there's no money in ideas. And that may not matter to you because I too know very well that a stonking idea is, on occasion, better than sex. In fact, the people who live for ideas are having ideas sex. With themselves.

Idea after idea after idea. In waves.

They can't stick to any one idea before they've come up with another. The inference is that the newer idea is always the better one, but it isn't. It's just different.

There's no money in ideas. **The money's in the implementation of your idea.**

And yes, all of us ideas people dream of being paid for our ideas and many of us are, in different ways. I have a client right now whose goal is to be paid for her ideas and she has the greatest chance of success at that as anyone I've ever seen because she has plenty of career cred to bring to her ideas work. And she's putting her back into it too, experimenting, finding her feet, feeling the frustration and carrying on anyway. She will prevail.

But here's the choice for the rest of us.

Do you want to make a living employing yourself for money doing the ONE thing (for now) that you love? Yes? Good! Then pick that one thing and get going and I don't want to hear from you with any new ideas until you've made that one work. Any ideas you do have must be corralled and applied to the One Thing, or parked in a notebook/treasure chest for later. Once you get used to channelling all your sexy ideas into your current project, it fills the same need I promise you. I do that now. It only works.

If that doesn't sound like you, then you aren't going to make any money at this self-employed, work-at-home lark. But you are going to have a lovely life having ideas sex. With yourself. Go for it. Fill your boots. Who am I to stand in the way of you and yet another sexy idea?

One final thought and thanks go to my coaching colleague Margaret Collins for this. Serial focus. It doesn't mean you can't do all your ideas, it just means you can't do them all at once. Do one, make it work. Do the next one, make it work. Do the one after that, make it work. Serial focus.

One person can only do one thing at a time if she's to do it well. One idea is a full-time business for you and me.

Or, as Steve Nobel once said to me, if you chase two rabbits you'll catch neither. That's all you need to know on this topic.

PS There's another reason for not living in the ideas sex shop all day every day and it is this, sent in specifically for this book: *"the crazy creative part of my brain that generates so many ideas from one spark, that it leaves me incapable of following any of them because of the mental tornado they create."*

They create a mental tornado. They leave you incapable of following any of them. How painful. How incapacitating. **Stop it immediately.**

NOTES

- **What personal system will you adopt to corral and queue all of your wonderful ideas?**
- **How will you train yourself to streamline all your cracking ideas to be of benefit to the One Thing you are working on right now?**
- **What other ways are there for you to enjoy all your creativity without the cacophony/mental tornado knocking you off course?**

Question 34

IS IT OK TO TALK OPENLY ABOUT MY SPIRITUALITY?

"People will think I'm a whack job!"

For the longest time, I was a bit too circumspect about this, fearing the whack job diagnosis myself. And I know some of my friends and family and colleagues and clients do not agree with a lot of my own spiritual and esoteric beliefs. If anything, that just serves to strengthen them. I know what's true for me. Also, my beliefs are visceral or as my friend Susie-From-Manchester would say "I just knowed it, Miss." Other people spouting on about theirs, where we are not in agreement, just makes mine strengthen. It's like mental and spiritual muscle toning by resistance training, in effect. Does that even make sense? I don't speak gym.

I have also become - shock, horror! - what only a couple of years ago I myself would have called a conspiracy theorist.

As you know, I call it woo woo. I shouldn't really. It's somewhat derogatory, but it's a name I adopted when I was sitting in uncertainty about how much and how many of my beliefs I would share with the wider world, and how far I should go with outing myself. Woo woo was shorthand, if you will. It gave me a name to call it, taking it lightly.

With my clients, I usually find out early on whether or not they too are woo woo. If they are, no problem, we are on the same page and many of them, men and women, have picked me precisely for that reason. If you follow that logic, the more out I am about it, the more successful I become. Like attracts like. Memorably, one of my clients found me by Googling "I AM ABUNDANCE" and discovering me on the front page.

With my pals who don't share my beliefs I am perhaps more circumspect, but these are often brilliant brainy academics or scientists who went to the UK's finest universities and they don't believe in the esoteric and are mainly too polite to tell me that, or we simply don't discuss it; it's easier that way.

But people constantly surprise me. A new client will, for instance, use the word "energy" in our first call and that tips me the wink about his beliefs and then I can open up with mine too. Those who don't, I offer them what I believe and slowly they laughingly and lovingly adopt one or two concepts for themselves too. Even my most sceptical friend was amazed to discover she could magic up a black cab in the dark and rainy London night, something she used to believe was impossible, or a convenient parking space in pole position, at will. But we woo woos know those are both too easy, right? Woo woo 101.

I watch other spiritual people I love and follow like, say, Martha Beck and Wayne Dyer, talking openly about their spiritual beliefs and I notice the rise and rise (and rise) of how many people are interested in exploring all the New Agey content we believe in and love. I suspect from your use of the word spiritual you are perhaps taking this a tad - and a step - more seriously even than me.

I think it must have been very satisfying to have been Louise Hay who brought us all of this stuff through her publishing empire and asked us to take much of it on trust initially. We gravitated towards it because it spoke to us, not because we were brainwashed. Today, Hay House put on their stages people who have been teaching us stuff for decades and which scientists are now beginning to prove.

Some people need that scientific proof and, strangely, it is now catching up with woo woo. Where on earth have they been and what took them so long?!

Clearly, most people are still suspicious and remain sceptics. I couldn't give a hoot really. I believe what I believe and I know what's true in my own life and I've done my own experiments and I know what works for me from some quite mild stuff which you could put down to coincidence, to some really whacky stuff about healing my relationship with my parents after their deaths. And other bereaved souls have shared their similar experiences too, so I know I am not alone. Not that that would bother me either.

I don't really care what people think, I guess that's what it boils down to. We are all somewhere along this scale from zero to 100% and we are mostly happy with our place on that scale otherwise we'd move. Some have open minds. Some respect your choices though wouldn't adopt them necessarily as their own. And that's fine. Those of my clients who take up that space nevertheless know and are inclined to say things like "My coach/Judith would say…" and that means it's in their awareness. I am content with that.

I am drawn to the spooky, the woo woo and the whack-jobs. I love whack-jobs, me. The wackier the better. I wish there were more in the world. Many geniuses have been written off as whack-jobs, either fairly or unfairly. That's just life. People are fearful of what they don't understand, but none of this has ever scared me. All it's ever done is resonated with my inner knowing, reassured me, stood up (or not) to my own accidental or purposeful experiments, and drawn others like me to me. All good so far, am I right?

Talk openly about anything you like and, in so doing, inspire and encourage others to be brave too. I think you'll find a warmer audience than perhaps you fear. At the very least, those who disagree or disapprove will still love you and respect your choices. And I, for one, would march on Westminster to protect your right to draw inspiration from wherever you darn well please and talk about it openly too.

Do it to encourage others, but only to the extent that you are happy doing so. Inch by inch. And, as you discover that the sky isn't falling in, another inch.

Society is often harsh on those with whom we don't agree because we fear what we don't understand. Recently someone told me that one of the actresses I really like is a Scientologist. I'll confess it made me think a little bit differently about her, but not of her acting work which is, and will always remain, totally great to me whatever she believes in her private life which is none of my business, frankly.

I am thinking too of the Jehovah's Witnesses. We all make fun of them when they come to the door. I always pretend I am too busy working to talk to them. Thank God (!) for entry phones. But they don't stop trying to convert us and society more than tolerates them. They do no harm to anyone with their beliefs, or not to my eyes anyway. This is all simply a matter of opinion and personal choice.

Initially, I'd recommend only opening up to those who you trust with your tenderest of tender stuff and, as life goes on, be prepared to draw to you more and more like minds and hearts. There's me, for starters!

PS After I wrote this, I had a quick squint at FB. You and I are going to have to seriously up our game if we want to compete with the whack-jobs on there! Nothing to do with spirituality, just whack-jobs. I like that word. I like typing it. I shall start using it more.

NOTES

- When it comes to your own beliefs about spirituality or politics or anything, to what extent do you keep quiet or share your views with the world?
- Thanking about that now, what would you change?
- Is that set in stone, or might you change your mind in the future?

Question 35

WHAT ARE YOUR BEST TIPS FOR BETTER WORKING WITH MY BUSINESS PARTNER WHO IS ALSO MY HUSBAND, ESPECIALLY WHEN WE DON'T SEE EYE TO EYE?

My client co-owns a business with her husband in which they both work. She feels the division of labour is unfair and resentment builds up and then explodes. Her partner doesn't like his list of jobs increasing. He doesn't really see the problem and is reluctant to talk about it.

She feels misunderstood especially in the amount of her own workload and commitment to the business. The burden falls on her for dealing with people, computer work, admin and accounts which she's tried to get his help with but it wasn't being done accurately and then it took her longer. Often she had to wait on him before she could do her part which just made it easier to do it all herself. The time she spends doing "invisible" work is not appreciated and not given the same kudos as his work that can more easily be seen.

"What's the best way to keep patient when negotiating especially when tired, and when things don't look like they are going to change? And how do you negotiate when you feel on the back foot, when your partner doesn't really understand or seem interested in the work you're doing?"

Hmm. A couple of thoughts. Firstly, my client and I know each other quite well and we share a lot of personality traits, nearly-OCD and a liking for both control and things being done properly, i.e. our way LOL. I have talked to her about the possibility of outsourcing bits of her workload and getting some local help with the hard-labour physical bits of it so that she has more time for the office and admin and marketing and accounting type of task, but this isn't easily possible due to the employment rules and regs in the country where she lives and also to her relative geographical remoteness.

But I noticed for the first time when I was reading this that there are some things which could perhaps be outsourced from the office work and done remotely by a VA. Which means her other half has a choice, to do them himself or have the business pay for them to be done so that my client has an easier life.

In a two-person business, usually the workload cannot be identical, but as far as possible I think you must try and organise it so that the workload is of **equal value** to the business and to your relationship.

The strength of any partnership is your chalkiness and cheesiness, your yin and yang. There would be no point in both of you being identical or capable in the same ways. The ship is just top heavy then. You have to find ways to play to your respective strengths, get your workload to feel equal or equal-ish and then outsource everything else as far as possible.

The E-Myth Revisited by Michael Gerber has a good system for this, where two brothers write down what roles they will each play in their business and include things in that list that they are prepared to do for now but not forever. And they sign off on that pledge until such time as the business can find other ways to get that done. I'd definitely be re-reading the book and trying to get that organised in your business.

Next, I'd be trying to sort out a means of clear and clean and frequent communications. By this I mean don't let anything build up and fester. Ever. It is so much worse then and leads - as you say - to explosions. I don't want you to be so tired either so, for me, that has to be a priority, getting more and better quality rest. You've been at this business long enough now to find ways to do that for sure. Start-ups are different, though they don't need to be either, frankly. But they are.

Clear and clean communications are so much easier when you learn how to communicate well, how to speak openly about how you feel without blaming or pointing the finger. Another human being doesn't make you feel anything, you decide how you feel about their behaviour and what they say. Learn how to ask for your own needs to be met, or his proposals for firstly seeing it as important because you do even though he doesn't agree, that's just respect by the way, and then helping the two of you to find a solution for the business which will also benefit your relationship. Perhaps that's the carrot? Who wants a wife who is tired all the time??

I think different personality types have to be recognised and appreciated. You have come into each other's lives for a reason, learn whatever those messages are. You could learn to relax more often and more easily, he could learn to be more efficient now and again. And people who love one another try to get this right for the sake of that love, though none of us roundies can or should ever try to squeeze ourselves into a square box just to appease, when negotiation is still on the table.

Appreciate what you do have.

Count your blessings.

Love and accept yourself and each other exactly as you are.

Love and boundaries and confusion arising therefrom are hard enough in a relationship, let alone in a business. I used to know lots of life partners who worked together in business. I find I only know one or two now and that would be worth exploring, wouldn't it? Who do we know who's in business successfully with their other half and what tricks have they learned that we can borrow?

But I have always known business partners - two male friends, two female friends or one of each - whose common interests brought them together. And the dramatic tension of their differences made their businesses great. For a while. Then the human beings that they were couldn't hack it anymore. And their different personality types or values tore them asunder. I'm am not being overly dramatic here for the sake of the tale. As their accountant, I saw and was involved in some very very painful partnership splits, and in some of those splits the dramatis personae never recovered their original friendships before it became too late, and that's a terrible price to pay.

Sometimes the very thing that draws us together, attracting opposites, which is so good for all types of relationships, all too soon drives us bonkers and apart in the end. Try to appreciate his cheesiness to your chalkiness, and vice versa. Try to organise it so that matters are fair and of equal value as far as possible. Set up a formal system for airing grievances and addressing them together as business partners, Mr & Mrs CEO of Your Biz PLC, and not as husband and wife. Don't take business "home", even if you live there, so that's another boundaries opportunity.

You will get good at this in time. I think you are comparing his output to yours and finding him wanting and clearly, from your description, that's the truth as well as your opinion. Address the truth, the business problem, a.s.a.p. and don't punish him for being different from you. Vive la différence! You are a grafter. He isn't. Your style isn't better than his, it's different, that's all. Yes, I can quite imagine why it gets on your wick, but would you want to change the man you fell in love with?

I've seen couples split up over less. I don't see this happening to you; your personal lives are too great together, which means happily that this is purely and simply a business problem, so treat it as such and deal with it only during office hours. If you keep looking for solutions to the problems the business has, you will find them. If you keep trying to change your husband to be more like you wish perhaps that he was, more like you, that's not a path I'd recommend or follow myself. If men were more like us, we wouldn't love them or fancy them. End of. That's a path fraught with the very worst type of dangers. Don't go that route unless you are absolutely sure you have no alternative. I can see many, many choices for you, many sledgehammers to crack this nut when all you two need is a few little taps. Speaking of tapping, have you tried EFT on these feelings? That would help enormously. Once the feelings are out of the equation, I sense that the business solutions will simply present themselves.

Good luck! I know you can do this.

PS Since writing this about a month ago, my client has let me know that magic and miracles have opened up in this scenario with her husband expressing a willingness to do something that neither of us ever thought we'd see. Which just goes to show that any of us can change anything whenever we want.

The E-Myth Revisited by Michael Gerber, subtitled Why Most Small Businesses Don't Work and What To Do About It is required reading if you have the sort of business which would benefit from systems. Even if you don't, or don't think you have, do read it anyway. Even though it is a tad outdated, it speaks to how we got ourselves in such a mess in the first place. I shall make no apologies in recommending this book more than once, or reminding you to re-read it when you have forgotten its lessons. It is an easy read, the story of Sarah and her pie shop. I wish I had read it BEFORE I sold my accountancy business, not after! And, if you like it, there's a version of the E-Myth for everyone these days: Managers, Accountants, Contractors, Dentists, Physicians, Attorneys, Architects, Optometrists. You name it, MG has adapted his book to fit your profession. Ka ching!

Question 36

WHY DO I ALWAYS PUT MY OWN SELF-CARE LAST?

Without you, your business is nothing. So your top priority always is looking after you because you are both your business's finest asset and its worst liability. When anything threatens your health and well-being, you cannot work and your income dries up or your business comes under threat in other ways.

This is called self-care, and because we are so poor at prioritising it we need to think of it as Extreme or Radical. We need always to focus on it **first and foremost** and what we tend to do is leave it to last. If there are a few moments left for us at the end of the week we are lucky and tend to collapse on the sofa with a glass of wine. This probably isn't the solution we are looking for!

Successful people do it first. They *do* prioritise it. Consequently their outcomes in their business and their work reflect this.

So let's work out how that might go for you.

First of all, we need to work out what are your non-negotiables when it comes to getting some tiger in the tank.

For me, it would be…lots and lots of peace and quiet and alone time. Plenty of good quality sleep. Enough top-notch input in terms of reading and watching to stimulate my creativity and inspire me, and the complete avoidance of all dramatic and annoying people. The removal of the wrong people is always top of my list and something I police religiously. Ah, and I remember… NO TELEPHONES! I don't do phones because they are noisy and they interrupt my peace and solitude at the agenda of the caller. Skype or Zoom or Webex by appointment or permission, that's me.

You see how easy it is to choose and regulate what helps you to feel happy and which keeps you in the zone?

For most of my clients, this would involve some form appreciation of the great outdoors, and perhaps exercise too even if only walking the dog or taking the kids to school on foot and collecting them later in the same way. I cannot think of a single problem which isn't solved in the short term at least by either physical exercise or deep breathing, and physical exercise has the same effect of oxygenating us in a way which tends to see the bad shiz be gone rather efficiently.

Step away from the computer. Get a life.

Pursue your hobbies and interests, however bonkers. In fact, the more bonkers the better here because we tend not to be able to help the things we love, we are just inexplicably drawn towards them. I had a lovely time the summer before last doing some of that adult colouring and I am thinking of taking it up again, I slightly miss it. I am a colourful person and it brought more colour and more relaxation into my life in a double-whammy.

I find swimming and showers, anything in water to be both restful and creatively stimulating. Lots of genius ideas come to me when I am in or near water.

Many swear by running and the gym.

You could do worse than look up Hal Elrod's Miracle Morning process and although I don't know anyone who started it who has kept it up, I certainly do not rule it out. His prescription is SAVERS - for Silence, Affirmations, Visualisation, Exercise, Reading and Scribing.

Daily journaling or Morning Pages, they're ace. Morning Pages come from a book by Julia Cameron called The Artist's Way. I never finished the book. Morning Pages were all I needed to learn about, but you may find the entire book useful for your creative biz too.

These days I like to go for a drive to get myself into a trance. I've always loved driving and now I find it oddly therapeutic. That's how I came up with the idea for this book!

What else? Oh yes, meditating of course. Pilates and Yoga.

And music is a real mood changer and vibe raiser, as is a Skype call with me for many of my clients.

Now, look... don't be a muppet with this. You don't have to do all of these and, no doubt, I've left your favourites off this list. Make your own list and keep it in a place where you can see it easily in your home office. Refer to it daily and find a way to do a couple of the items on it or as many as you can, and do it first.

Make a habit of one or two and stick to them without fail. Do not let even hell or high water come between you and your weekly choir practice, or whatever's your bag.

Look for the things that make you feel good and do a whole lot more of them.

Remember what Gandhi is reputed to have said. On a busy day, double the dose. When you are feeling low, do more of it. And when you don't feel up to working, leave your desk and go and do some of the things on your self-care reminder list, or absolutely nothing at all. I find a nap to be uniquely restorative. Everything feels better when I am well rested.

You might also incorporate some affirmations and woo woo into your daily routine. Gratitude for starters. There's a real game-changer for you and, even if that's all you do, your life will metamorphose and you'll never slide back for as long as you keep up the daily practice.

That's the key. You are making and keeping and committing to a daily practice. Don't overdo it. Pick the thing that if you just get it done every day makes everything else go with a swing. And if the only time for you to do it is before everyone else gets up in the morning, make that unbreakable commitment to yourself.

Build in buffer zones. If you are travelling, work out how much time you need before and after to prepare and recover. My clients endlessly underestimate the toll that travelling through many time zones has on our bodies. I do not. Once bitten, twice shy.

This is your job and only yours, to put the oxygen mask on. And put it on first. Then everything just flows and, when and if it doesn't, you can manage and cope for the duration because you have plenty of stores of feel-good to get you through.

There is a Zen quote (see mention of Gandhi above) that goes something like "Meditate for an hour every day unless you are too busy. In that case, meditate for two hours."

In summary, your job is to find a daily spiritual or secular practice, any practice that makes you feel good.

1. Do it every day without fail.
2. When under pressure double your efforts.

You are SO going to thank me for this one. It only makes EVERYTHING work. When my clients do it, their results are outstanding. When they come, apparently having fallen out of their zone of genius, I ask what's happened with the daily routine and the answer is they stopped doing it because it was working! Doh.

NOTES

1. **Find your daily practice of self-care. What will it be? What prescription will you write yourself?**
2. **Keep adjusting until you find the thing which as long as you do it every day allows everything else to just flow.**
3. **Never stop doing it.**
4. **When you notice life has turned to pants, did you stop doing the thing? I told you... NEVER stop doing it! What are you like?**

BREATHING SPACE – CHAPTER FIVE - PERSONAL

In Chapter Five we have looked at having a lovely life and not feeling bad about that, enjoying lots of sexy ideas and how to corral them usefully in your creative projects, training yourself to be more productive in creating your biz your way, spirituality and how much to share about that, getting along with life and business partners and putting ourselves and our self-care at the very top of our intentions, not leaving ourselves till last.

What did you notice? Any aha moments or realisations for you?

Remember, there's nothing wrong with you, you are perfect exactly as you are and you are mostly making up any bonkersness that you might have to keep it interesting. Having your life and your biz go your way is possible. Make a plan today to have that download into your reality as soon as you like. What would it look like, I wonder?

Here's some space for that dreaming first off. Then next you'll turn it into plan. Then into your own personal unique gorgeous reality.

Write it all down here or somewhere else. Or draw it or record it somehow. Just daydream it. It all counts. Then set some intentions. Then live them. This is going to be easy. There's a great intention for starters! Have that one on me.

Don't forget to pay attention to inklings and tiny thoughts and feelings. Sometimes your intuitive nudges can be really small and quiet, like the still small voice inside struggling to be heard. Get quiet. It's always there. You can tune in to your higher self or inner guidance sat nav whenever a divine inspiration is called for, which is most of the time in my world.

Less effort, more ease.
What else would you like less or more of?

CHAPTER SIX

Philosophy

Question 37

WHY DO I FEEL BAD THAT MY WORK ISN'T EITHER HARD ENOUGH OR SUFFICIENTLY WORTHY OR INTELLECTUAL?

Self-employment feels too easy to my client; it's all dropping into her lap.

Hard work was hard wired into me at birth. And it is worthy, it really is. I ran my life and my accounting business according to the principles of hard work once upon a time* and guess what? It only works! But it isn't The Way. It's just one of the ways.

When I am tired and not thinking straight and I want to get something done, I fall back on these principles, that old well-worn groove, and hard work gets it done. Hard wired. Told ya.

But now I have woken up and discovered I am 62. And once I got over that shock... here's the thing. Even after I sold my first business in 1997 and I wasn't yet nearly as old as 62, just 42 in fact, I already knew that I didn't want to use those same principles of Hard Work in the next chapter of my life or career either, 'cos hard work had nearly finished me off. I can do it if called upon, but it is only one setting on the Judith-o-meter and I've discovered that there are LOADS of other settings to choose from. Who knew?

Everything's a choice, and wouldn't you rather have it be easy? Light and easy?

My current favourite saying in this regard is "When it's right, it's easy" and I honestly believe that. Pushing uphill for the sake of it, and struggle, well OK if that's your only setting or you insist on it being hard, but check your upbringing and your conditioning and see where that comes from. Examine it under a useful spotlight. No blame involved, just understanding.

And with one bound you can be free. No, I'll be honest. It takes a few more goes than just one bound, but it can be done. I know. I've done it.

Let's look now at worthy. And intellectual.

Yep, I get a buzz out of intellectual. Always have, always will, I flatter myself I've got a brain like that. But it doesn't mean I don't enjoy all sorts of silly nonsense too, in fact I find anti-intellectual to be quite relaxing. I cannot take it as far as reality TV where they really want the contestants to bonk each other on primetime, but I can take it as far as page-turning light crime novels with a heroine who makes me feel good about myself, written by a woman employing herself for money who is never going to win the Nobel Prize for Literature but who is meeting a need in a reader like me and who is very clearly enjoying herself enough to create a prodigious output. AND making a LOT OF DOSH. Her books sell fabulously well and she writes lots of them, luckily for me.

Oh, she also gives the lie to worthy too.

You can bust this particular bonkersness yourself by looking at the things in life that you enjoy. Are they all hard, worthy and intellectual or are lots of them light and easy and fun and pleasurable and entertaining?

Same applies to work, business and self-employment, Old Love. And to doing something that you love for money. I know you know this because since submitting this question, although no doubt a part of your psyche still feels and believes it to some dwindling extent, I have seen you start to discover precisely how light and easy and fun can also = dosh!

*Denotes fairy-tale made-up bonkersness which is very persuasive as it seeps into our consciousness and becomes "truth".

NOTES

- Set aside some time to examine your beliefs. Which ones are working for you and which ones have you simply inherited, not yet taken the time to explore and reinvent? Bust the bonkersness! Go on, you have my permish.
- What does go well and easily, and how much more of that could you stand? Invite it in.
- What do you struggle with and why? How much longer will you choose struggle?

Question 38

WHEN IS ENOUGH ENOUGH?

Oh! I **so** agree with you. I know you and I both know when enough is enough. And we are both quite or very close to that place where we appreciate that we are enough, we have enough, and we know enough.

Gentle Reader, my questioner is a consultant but she also does another couple of funky and interesting things on the side. She's not my only consultant client and there's often a somewhat tricky quandary that goes with being a consultant which my freelancer readers will also recognise.

When we have a contract we are grateful to have it and are mostly well paid, or at least thankful we have money coming in. Between contracts, we sigh with relief because we have, at least initially, money in the bank so we can pursue our own other interests which are usually many and varied. But depending on how long that "between contracts" goes on, we can begin to allow scarcity to creep in. Cash reserves are dropping and we are not sure yet when or if we will get another contract. Which, in turn, means that when we are in a contract, we never know when is the right time to give it up if it doesn't end naturally, or give us up.

Or, to put it another way, when is enough enough? I know my client's question is broader than this but I am restricting it to just this for now. It's a right old to do, isn't it? And yet, it isn't. It's just the natural ebb and flow which goes with the territory of being freelancer or a contractor.

In the early days of working for ourselves, we tend to grab whatever's offered. Before we get it, we pine for it and fear for our savings dropping to zero or below. We are relatively indiscriminate. Then we start the contract and we see what's wrong with it and we determine to choose more wisely next time, assuming all other things are equal. Which they never are, of course.

If we go back to my theory that we don't die when we run out of money and that it always comes from somewhere, then we can afford to hold out a bit longer, until we get what we really want and deserve.

Some of my clients who are good at manifesting, as this particular Top Bird is, can easily be more abundant than others. They know their perfect contract is just waiting for them in divine escrow. And all of my clients get to that place in the end, after a few terrifying false starts.

Another client asked me a question only this week about how she should afford something she wanted. She's another contractor as it happens. I said to her, because I know she's spooky, that if she was meant to have it then she would magically manifest it and not to rule that out. Within 48 hours she wrote again to let me know that was precisely what had happened; yep, no surprise to me, Beloved. She'd booked the initial session of the thing that was her heart's desire, and one of her contracting companies had been in touch to say they wanted her back for a nice long period of time and at a higher rate than her current contract which runs out fairly shortly. So now she knows she has the extra cash to pay for the lovely thing.

Enough is a little bit of a movable feast. My enough may be a lot less than yours, for instance. It certainly is when it comes to things. There's almost nothing I want. And yet, did you know, it is almost impossible to manifest more money?

So I tend to say woo woo things out loud to the Big U like "If you think I need more money, please send me more clients." And they tend to show up. Ka-ching.

Also, your sense of enough changes at different stages of your life.

As you learn over the years of employing yourself for money that you will always survive, whatever happens, that you will thrive frequently too and that ebb and flow is natural, then you will come to see that we always have enough. Sufficiency is a beautiful thing.

Just for now, what constitutes enough?

Question 39

WHAT'S THE BEST WAY TO AVOID COMPROMISING MY FREEDOM?

Earlier this summer, my client was negotiating a Big Contract. This was going to be quite a commitment for her and involve her in working with a few sub-contractors too, but it was what we'd been talking about and the sort of income she had been desiring and taking steps towards and following up leads and going to meetings in order that she would manifest precisely that; a big chunk of work and cash. Her intentions became her reality.

And next, her immediate fear was that the new juicy Big Contract would limit her freedom, that most precious of precious reasons why most of us become self-employed. Her concern was that it might compromise that freedom.

But she was still at the contract negotiation stage and a contract doesn't close unless both parties get what they want out of it. So she still had the power to negotiate how she would deliver the work. She could work from home and only go into her client's offices for vital meetings of a certain nature. They couldn't come to expect anything else if a precedent was set from the get-go and she stuck to her guns and exercised her boundaries, all tasks in which I shall support her. She will still be free to travel and do her work remotely. She could, if she wanted, write into the contract that she would do the work at midnight wearing a pink hat while living in Ibiza.

We seem to forget how much power we have in every negotiation when we are self-employed, at least initially when a newbie and, to some extent, that never goes away as we always lose perspective when too close to any particular aspect of our work and business.

No one can ever take away your personal power except that you surrender it to them.

You always have the power. (You always have The Power too.)

Another story illustrates this rather nicely. When I asked my Club 100 for contributions to this book, one client replied as follows.

Client: *What immediately comes to mind is the big block I was giving myself on our call this month about needing loads of clients, and at the same time worrying that that would mean I didn't have time to write my own stuff. Then you pointed out that I actually only needed a few clients, and that still gave me time for my own writing. We took off the brakes, and within 2 weeks I have a new client.*

Me: *"took off the brakes", love it.*
Client: *You said it!*

We have power and choice and freedom at all times, both as human beings and as people who employ ourselves for money. Sometimes, in both places, that's compromised for all sorts of reasons. But mostly it isn't. Don't give away your power. Pay attention. Do not allow it to be taken from you either. If any contract has draconian terms on the other side to which you are not prepared to agree, then don't. By saying no to the wrong things, you leave room for the right.

- **Where are you putting the brakes on in your own biz and what's your underlying fear?**
- **What might happen if you simply lift that foot a little, or a lot?**

Question 40

WHY DO I KEEP SELF-SABOTAGING AND SLOWING DOWN MY OWN PROGRESS?

What do you do when you have a major #1 project which is very important to you, paramount even, but LIFE STUFF keeps on getting in the way?

This is something I see my clients do. And, for sure, we all have varied and interesting and busy, even full, lives. And what I try to get them to do, not always successfully, is to see two things.

- How to prioritise and say no to stuff that gets in the way
- See that what they let in must be at least as important as their #1 project, if not more so, or they have self-sabotaged. They have given away time they can't get back.

This can take quite a long time to retrain. If you've always been a Nice Girl or Guy and you have - let's say - a significant other with a family, you have a family too, and/or you have a child or three between you, or maybe you have to do some paying work on the side while you are getting up and running so that you can pay your bills. Or maybe all of the above plus you are quite sociable and so you get out and about, occasionally coming home with a hangover which disables your precious working time tomorrow. Add into the mix that just like everyone else, you are sometimes poorly or burned out or both. You can't say no to any invitation, be it for work or fun. We know that your getting out and about is good but you occasionally do too much of it and all of this busyness and confusion just eats into your project time. Phew! It's all rather breathless, isn't it?

Either you must say no to more, or you have to realise that the fruition of your dream scenario is going to be a long time coming. It will take as long to come as the amount of other people's priorities and even self-ish fun you allow to go to the front of your queue, and we all do that occasionally for the healthy work-life balance. God, I HATE that expression but you know what I mean. Having a life. Enjoying that life. Being a human being not just a human doing.

Ask yourself before saying yes to ANYTHING else - is this more important to me that my #1 project? If not, it HAS to be a no. For now, not forever.

My friend Daphne-Who-Writes-Books taught me almost everything I know about this. At certain stages of the book-writing process, she simply said no to all invitations to go out to lunch or for coffee or to the cinema. Her writing career was more important to her, and she took it seriously. She did (and still does) have a significant other and I imagine she did make time for that relationship because it was at least as important to her as her books and her writing. I was less important and, although that stung, she trained me to know that between books she would be available for all sorts of hijinks and happy to have the fun distractions in her downtime. But that they would have to wait. For now, not forever.

Only you can decide what's more important than your lovely thing. But if you keep turning up in my diary and inbox, citing an endless list of distractions which you have allowed to get in the way of your project AGAIN, then it is clearly time to do some sorting, some prioritising, some saying no and explaining why, and some defining of boundaries.

Once you understand that this is you slowing yourself down and limiting your successful results from the very thing you told me that you live to do, then you'll realise that the problem begins and ends with you. And yes, you will worry about how to get all the needs of the different parts of you met, and about upsetting other people. But it isn't forever, it's just for now. So you can move faster to launch and to results and achievement, to feel-good.

So here's my tip. When people ask (or your alter ego wants) you to go and do stuff BEFORE your Top Priority, then buy yourself a little space first. You are changing your behaviour, perhaps the habits of a lifetime, so start by inserting an extra stage as Step One. Say to self and others "Let me get back to you on that once I've worked out how it fits in with my work schedule and my other diary commitments". Buy yourself a couple of hours or a couple of days. Sit with the invitation for as long as it takes you to work out if it is really more important than your Top Thing, then say yes. If it is less important or of equal importance, say no to the former and yes to only a very few of the latter.

This goes beyond just this question by the way. If in doubt, buy time. Sit with it. Allow the answer to bubble up. Don't rush to over-respond. Wait. Breathe.

I will keep pointing this out to you week after week and month after month, that your project will be forever in the making, and you will only be able to do fewer of your own beautiful personal projects in your lifetime and that may be just how you like it. But, if it isn't, then only you can say no to the things that are slowing you down.

This probably isn't a **Stop It Immediately** opportunity unless you want overnight change. It's probably more of a suck-it-and-see thing, an experiment one-day-at-a-time thing, until you are proficient at evaluating and prioritising and putting yourself and your projects first or first equal.

For some parents (or children of parents) there will be times in your life when you are unable to put yourself first or even first equal, and this is just as it should be because the health and well-being of others are at stake, sometimes even a matter of life and death. But once that stage of your life is over, and it will be all too soon, then you go back to putting yourself first. And attaining a balance in that too so you are not All Work and No Play. That just makes you dull, and that won't benefit your creative project either.

As with everything, it's finding the balance. The emotional squidginess here comes from either not knowing what's important and how to carve out that time for it and not taking yourself seriously yet, or being more concerned about the feelings of others who make requests of your time than you are of your own project. Yep, it's true. Your actions are speaking louder than your words. Only you can decide. I keep saying that because it really is the point of this one, but I'll bet the contents of my piggy bank you know when you are doing it and that it's getting rather painful too. So your opportunity is just to exercise more choice and willpower about all the temptations which come into your life. That power is yours, always was and always will be.

NOTES

- **What's really important to you, your #1 priority project?**
- **How can you make time and space for it in your busy life?**
- **What's gotta give, for now?**

Question 41

IS THERE SOMETHING WRONG WITH ME?

"There must be something wrong with me/my business model/what I'm doing because I haven't been able to make my business work. I feel embarrassed that I've not been able to make this work yet."

I read something very interesting last night in what is fast becoming a fave book by Pam Grout called Thank & Grow Rich. It was about the voice we use to talk to ourselves, and the nasty messages we tell ourselves too. Pam describes "the maniac in our own heads". She says a non-stop voice loop reminds her of all that's lacking in her life and this obnoxious voice keeps tabs on all she's doing wrong and makes long lists of things she needs to improve.

The voice is very clear that something is wrong with her.

For the longest time, she thought this voice *was* her because it did a very convincing impersonation. And it wasn't until she began counting her blessings that the other frequency was able to make contact, the still, small voice that whispered kind truths. It suggested that the most important thing Pam could do for herself was to **get happy and quit judging herself.**

The still, small voice reminds us that everything we see, everything we believe, is just a story we made up. Pam recommends that it is time to give our mind a new job.

I know my client who sent in this question knows this because she is a clever woman. I was reading Pam's book just as the question came in and I knew it was the answer. I often receive answers even before I know the question but these debits and credits were simultaneous.

Feelings of embarrassment and of something being wrong with us is not the vibe from which we are going to attract what we want or achieve the results we seek. We all know this; surely we all know this now, don't we? We all have both voices, it is just that the beastly judgmental one is SO MUCH LOUDER than the still small one.

There's nothing wrong you, or with any of us. And there's absolutely no need to feel embarrassment. There isn't anyone reading this who hasn't felt this at one time or another or who won't again at another time; I had just such an incident over the weekend and another this morning! Be kinder to yourself, please.

It can all just take longer (much longer) than you think or want, especially when you keep shifting in every sense. But impatience with yourself is not the solution.

Choose instead, as much as possible, nurturing thoughts and feelings and create an attractive vibe of self-love. Find an ease about yourself and your business that you can communicate both directly and indirectly to your potential clients. Allow it to leak out of every pore. Be a woman in love with life and with herself and at ease in her skin. That's your job. Let it radiate in all that you are, all that you do, how you show up to help clients, on social media, in your newsletters and most importantly of all, how you think of yourself. This will require some mental conditioning to start with until you remember that this is just as much a truthful assessment of who and where you are as the other. I know without a shadow of a doubt that's true because I know you.

Yes, I think there are things we've all done to slow down our own progress. And, even while that may even look very attractive to the casual onlooker, it isn't how it feels on the inside at all, is it?

I suppose the ultimate truth is that self-employment is as far away from employment as it is possible to be, and if you are judging your progress and success or lack of either on the standards which are the only ones you know, brought with you from your old schooling and business career, then no wonder you are running this narrative in your head. Your opportunity with Your Biz Your Way is total freedom and, in that humongous space, we can each find our own sweet spot. Some drop into that overnight, others take longer. It is humongous, as I said, so sometimes it can take a while to find your comfy place, a bit like camping. Not that I would ever find a comfy place were I camping, but I can be a bit of a princess like that.

Just like my relatively new low-carb way of eating, where others are obsessed by my weight loss, this isn't a race or a competition. I've stopped counting and measuring, and so can you. Who on earth are we measuring ourselves against? A bit like joining the gym and erroneously assuming everyone else is looking at your unfit bod and judging, they are not. They are far too obsessed with the view of themselves in the mirror to waste any energy looking and thinking about you. So, no need for embarrassment either. **Stop it immediately!**

You can relax into this being your new way of life, one in which you please yourself, you do entirely what you want to do and what you love and you take the focus off achievement by all measures that worked in your old life but do not in your new. You will find new measures for this new way of being and they simply bear no comparison.

In fact, the ones you brought with you from your old employed life work less well in 2017 than I have ever seen them work, because we are all changing and evolving all of the time.

The truth is that lots of people are less successful than they think and feel they "ought" to be. But, again, what are you measuring this against? By what are you judging yourself? There's really no-one to compare yourself with out here in this reality because you are unique, and if you even try doing that you will fall into all sorts of misery traps like these.

There is no doubt in my mind that anyone can employ themselves for money. Getting the flow started is often the trickiest bit and can, for some, be the bit which takes longest. We are groping about in the dark, trying to find a way of being and working that suits us. We are working out what the world wants from us and what they will pay for.

We are distracted by all the received wisdom and we are trying to model ourselves on others who seem to have it cracked. They make it look effortless. And some of us, myself at the head of the queue here, do not like to be not good at things. That's one of the reasons why I loved line dancing because I could be the best in the class, but hated the gym because every time I got good, they made it harder for me. I need to feel good, not endlessly challenged. And yes, I know it means I was improving but what good is that if it never feels like it? You are making improvements like that in your business. It just doesn't look or feel like it yet, and knowing doesn't feel like enough.

We each have to find our own way. Sometimes, sure, that feels like that little game where you wiggle and wiggle and wiggle the thing about until the little silver ball drops into the hole. Time-consuming. Impossible. Endlessly challenging, up to a point! But everything we do and learn to do in this life takes time to finesse.

There's nothing wrong with you. You are on the journey. Maybe it is taking longer than it has taken some others of your acquaintance to get the magical silver ball in the hole, but comparisons are meaningless and soul-destroying. Energy zapping too. I know you are cast down by this often. I feel for you.

My recommendations would be to strip away all shoulds and sink into loves instead. I suspect the answer is right under your nose and when you eventually get the little silver ball into the hole you will exclaim in wonder about how you could have missed it for so long when it was so obvious and so close. That's what happened to me.

But only you can decide. I do firmly believe (and I know this is a tad woo woo for you, my client) that if you do what you love, the money will follow.

Trust yourself enough to do what you really love. And trust in the abundant universe who still has your back even while you feel you are floundering.

Let go.

Everything's unfolding perfectly just exactly as it is. You are having a more interesting journey than most. And yours and mine and everyone's are 100% unique.

There are no text book answers. We all just wiggle and wiggle and wiggle until it works. And as long as you keep trying and adjusting and focusing on what you love, you'll break through in the end. There's no failure except when we give up and, even then, who's to say you've failed except that horrid voice you've been conditioned to carry with you all your life?

***

As luck would have it, just as I was finishing this piece, artist Rhian Wyn Harrison sent me the following. Since she answered her own question I asked for her permission to share her Q&A in its entirety. And there you have it. She's wiser than she knows. How funny that she should share this right at this red hot second. And for it to be so precisely on this topic.

"One of the constants is when every painting goes through that "Oh God, this is shit" moment. Every. Single. Time. In the beginning, I used to just throw them away, but now I just push on past those thoughts, and on, until suddenly the painting works! I don't give up any more, but I am aware that I still think the work is no good. I think it is SO normal for creatives to self-judge and self-sabotage. I even believe that the edge of your seat tension between "it's fine" and "it's shit" is quite thrilling and ultimately breathes life into your creation. Does that make sense? I'm not sure if this is even a question now... but I would think it comes under the heading of "Am I good enough?"

Am I good enough? If that wasn't the original question, I don't know what was. And Rhian has been self-employed long enough to have discovered her own answer. She's getting the little silver ball in the hole despite the nasty voice still being audible. She's pushing on regardless, she knows this is normal. That's precisely what I wanted this book to do, to collect together thoughts about how normal we all are in our bonkersness and how we can do this anyway.

Thanks Rhian for helping me to make the case on this point. How wonderful to observe your advances and be able to share your wisdom in my book for the benefit of others.

NOTES

Look at Rhian's deliciously quirky art and see how she's doing: http://www.rhianwynharrison.com/

Read Pam Grout's wonderful book: Thank & Grow Rich: A 30-Day Experiment in Shameless Gratitude and Unabashed Joy published by Hay House.

Question 42

WHY DO I FEEL INFERIOR TO BETTER QUALIFIED ARTISTS?

I think this is a variant on what some of my more academic coaching colleagues might call Imposter Syndrome which almost everyone feels, by the way, especially women or so they tell me. If you don't know what IS is, please don't get distracted now and go rushing off to look it up, remember we don't need more information and you are already good enough, but…try on these few thoughts for size and see if they shift something for you.

My brother and I didn't go to University. It wasn't thought important in our family. Not our parents' fault really, neither of them had been and it wasn't necessarily the thing in our family in the early/mid-Seventies although all of the next generation did go and my brother married a woman who had been too.

He used to worry in the Eighties that perhaps he was inferior to his banking colleagues who had been to university, and he contemplated taking an MBA. Then he went on to work hard until he eventually became CEO of the bank he worked for man and boy, and that kyboshed that. It is entirely possible that couldn't be done or wouldn't work in today's world, where I believe university for 50% of the population was created just as a ruse to massage the unemployment figures and has now become a norm of sorts. An expensive norm. A wasteful norm.

My first career was as an accountant, as you know. And my second is as a coach. I have no formal qualifications in either, though forty years' experience at the coalface and lots of related study. You can go a long way without paper qualifications, as far as you decide to believe is possible. We all know many famous examples of this too. I won't name them, that's a bit of a yawn fest.

I am an entrepreneur. I don't believe in school. I've tried to suggest to various youngsters I know that they don't bother with further education type school either, certainly not if it means acquiring debt. Adult Ed is the thing. When you are ready and really want to study, you'll find a way. But going through it for the sake of going through it is a waste of all resources. If you love your subject and haven't left home before, you are as bright as a button, adore studying and are quite academic, then please ignore my opinions about university and further education and fill yer boots. And these remarks apply particularly to the UK. If you live elsewhere in the world it may be different, either better or worse.

I think work-related study while you are doing what you do is just as important. And I would never do that because other people thought I should, I would only do it for the sake of my own interest. Lots of my clients do it for the sake of their confidence, they feel more comfortable with a certificate. I don't, as it happens. Rather like Groucho Marx and, I think, Oscar Wilde, I don't want to belong to any club that would want me as a member. Rebel yell!

Just like running your own business is something learned while you do it, surely the same applies to being an artist? In fact, I know it is because I have a client who is an artist and I know precisely how much she's learned about the business of being an artist and about being a painter over the last few years. And I know who she's chosen to study with, in all the different areas of her work. And I know how much more confident she's become both as a human being and an artist as she's grown in that time. In fact, she's one of the best examples I know of changing as a person through being an artist and busting the inferiority bonkersness. Feel it if you must, and then go and do your arty (or any other type of) thing anyway.

You are a real artist. You were born an artist. I don't know by what criteria anyone would judge that anyway. Who says? Who do we believe? And why on earth do we swallow their codswallop?

I do remember hearing Ed Sheeran say on Jonathan Ross that his success as a musical artist only really started when he stopped trying to please other people and focused on what he wanted to write and perform. He says it even more effectively on Desert Island Discs too, so do catch up with that one if you haven't heard it. The BBC has a fabulous archive of almost everyone who's ever been on, and Ed was on just recently in 2017.

Now the remarkable thing about Ed is how self-assured he was about that from a very young age, much more so than most of us I think, especially those who are still battling these demons. I put that down to what must have been some ace parenting (both of his parents were artists and arty). The music industry adapted to him (not the other way around as is much more normal) as he went about his business of doing his music his way, he didn't sell out. He's his own man. It is just one of the reasons why I admire him, not to mention his creativity, productivity and financial successes.

And this is how it can be for you too if you just decide that it will be, and act accordingly.

Qualifications haven't been worth the paper they are written on in my own life. Other people, perhaps academics, would disagree, as would those who thoroughly loved their time at school or college or university. I know many people now who are going back to school at my age to get, for instance, creative MAs. Good on them, and I wouldn't rule that out for myself either. But I notice another one of your questions is about age. Bonkersness alert!

Rebel, and choose to be your own woman. You can go your own way (cue that wonderful Fleetwood Mac song of the same name, music being a real vibe raiser.) Surely this works in art more than any other area since beauty is in the eye of the beholder? Anything else is just snobbery, and people just generally being up themselves which they are wont to be.

If you like to read biographies for fun, I would seek out those by mavericks who didn't go to school and just went their own way about having a unique and successful creative life of their own design, without fear or favour. No comparisons! Perhaps you won't be the next David Hockney but you will be the first you.

And, if I were you, I'd keep painting and creating and showing and sharing and selling your work, proving to yourself how wrong this particular niggling bonkersness is. If you think about it, you've made it up, haven't you? Or bought into someone else's reality. **Stop it immediately!**

All the inspiration you could ever need from the Desert Island Discs archives and podcasts:
http://www.bbc.co.uk/programmes/articles/5qhJd1byxhTBYbSCFmw580y

You Can Go Your Own Way by Fleetwood Mac:
https://www.youtube.com/watch?v=6ul-cZyuYq4 - turn it up, sing it loud and unrepentantly

Question 43

WHY DOES HAVING THE RIGHT MINDSET FEEL LIKE A BIT OF A GAME?

"The sense that 'having the right mindset' is a bit of a game, and somehow I keep missing the ball because I've become distracted by any number of reasons."

Let's start with the word mindset. I don't like it, do you? It feels a bit jargony, a bit corporate. Yuk. I do remember where I was working as an accountant when I first heard it used daily and that was at a London recruitment agency where helping job applicants with their mindset was part of their brief. It always jarred with me, like fingernails down a blackboard.

I don't really feel I have a mindset, or that mine is the same or even similar to anyone else's. But to the extent that I understand what is meant by this word, I don't think of it as a game either. Although it must be said that I don't really like to think in terms of games or play. If you do, fill your boots although it doesn't sound from your question as though this is very helpful for you either?

Worst of all, for me, is the sense that a mindset can be wrong or right.

It is rare that I get up in the morning or ever, even way back at the start of my self-employment and consider what mindset to put on, as it were. I'm either in the mood for work, or I'm not. I'm either motivated, or I'm not.

If I have a mindset at all it is that I take myself reasonably seriously as a self-employed person who is out to support herself through her endeavour and enterprise. And also, over the years, I've learned to take that lightly too as I've come to understand that I'm not the only one in charge around these parts. So, sometimes, despite my best intentions it doesn't turn out as I plan, so I laugh because the only other alternative might be crying, and for sure there have been plenty of those days too.

But there's something in your question which freaks me a tad. The thing about mindset being a bit of a game. It isn't for me. But I can very much see how it would be possible to miss the ball and keep missing it due to the distractions that keep coming up.

And I think that is the sense in which we train ourselves to be good at working alone at home unsupervised. This morning is the last day of my summer holiday and my diary today says "Book" i.e. write some more. I'm getting close to the end now and I had wanted to finish it in August but took the last ten days off instead, much needed. So I am keen to get on with the book and had a big chunk of time in my diary for it today.

Lying in bed earlier and contemplating my day, and in view of a bad back, I remembered that writing my book is not improved by doing a long day, rather it is better done in 3-hour chunks so here I am at 09.35 and I've done my fannying and faffing about with emails and Facebook and I've shut them both now, intending to take myself seriously as a writer until lunchtime.

Is that a mindset? If so, that's not a game to me. I take myself seriously as a woman who supports herself through her delicious self-employment where, remember, I only do one thing. And who took August off from that, mostly to write a book. So I do not allow myself to become distracted all that much either.

I think this is probably a continuum and we each find our own place on it with time and training. That training is done by you. It is done by experimenting with what brings results. And if you can't do it all by yourself then you do it with an accountability buddy. You both agree you will do heads down uninterrupted work all morning without distractions of any description and, by such training and disciplines, more and better results are achieved and good working habits ingrained.

Sorry, I went all serious on you there for a bit.

In summary:

- Choose a friendlier word than mindset
- Find something sufficiently motivating, exciting or interesting to do that you cannot wait to get at it each day
- Take your work seriously especially if it is the source of your income, or even if it's not now that I come to think about it; you are an artist and, to the extent that I am a writer, let us both take ourselves seriously in those areas.
- Train yourself into good working habits so that distractions just fall away and catch yourself on quickly when you notice yourself doing the distraction thing
- Stop with the bonkersness, which you might do with a buddy or a coach

My client also shared "the sense that I know this is all nonsense, but still find myself acting as though I believe it" And I find myself wondering what would be a better and more empowering thought to take up.

NOTES

What beliefs about your lovely biz your way would support not undermine you?

BREATHING SPACE – CHAPTER SIX - PHILOSPHY

Chapter Six has been about matters philosophical. Do we need to work hard and be worthy and intellectual? What is enough? How can we protect our freedoms in self-employment, how are we slowing ourselves down with self-sabotage, and unhelpful feelings which can come at any time and in all shapes and sizes.

What did you notice? It's all in the noticing, Team. 'Cos then we can make up our minds to change our minds.

Notice too how much choice you have about everything you think and (almost) everything you do, and don't do.

Take a breather and jot down some thoughts. Return to this page at any time where revisiting this particular set of questions would be useful. Look at your notes later and see if they still make sense or if just noticing has liberated your bonkersness to leave town.

_____

_____

_____

_____

_____

CHAPTER SEVEN

Practical

Question 44

IN EMERGENCIES, WHAT SHOULD I FOCUS ON?

I think the short answer is the thing right in front of you.

The longer answer is what is the nature of the emergency? If the house is on fire, or you've hurt yourself or a member of your family is poorly, then you know what to do. Dial 999 and get the emergency services onto it.

If what you mean is in our businesses, then what sorts of emergencies are there?

- Deadlines
- Running out of money
- Threats various e.g. a solicitor's letter
- The government changing the rules endlessly and trying to catch you out with a fine
- What else?

Do you know the book by Stephen Covey called The 7 Habits of Highly Effective People in which he teaches us to make the distinction between urgent and important?

If you never make that distinction, everything will always be urgent or feel like an emergency. And many people run their lives like this, fire-fighting. The man who bought my first business operated like this. He had too much to do all the time, so he just did the most urgent. An awful way to live your life and run your business, little satisfaction and total and constant exhaustion. Burnout is your only destination.

If you tackle important, the number of urgent requests and emergencies tends to fall away or reduce dramatically. And your adrenaline levels return to healthy, giving you something in the tank for the inevitable real emergency every now and again. I cannot remember the last time I had a real emergency and that is all down to good planning, not doing stuff which is meaningless and having reserves mostly of time and energy. I create reserves of time by always being early to things such as meetings and my coaching calls with clients whenever possible, and also by overestimating how much time most things take. And then I create reserves of energy by resting up a lot, slowing down and thinking. I find that they complement each other beautifully. Over-estimating how much time something will take will often result in a surplus of time and spare resources which can then be reinvested in resting, even if it is only sitting quietly before a meeting and having a little think about a client or about my biz my way over a delicious cup of coffee. That also counts as extreme self-care which I've written about in answer to Q36. It's vital.

Most things take longer than they look like they will. One way to manage that is to charge more and take on less and build in enough time for everything in case things go wrong. It can take some time and some training to do this. So let's look at a few examples the sort of emergencies you might be thinking about.

Deadlines

They are very useful. Few of us would get much done if it weren't for a deadline, someone on our back waiting for us to deliver. I wouldn't want to be juggling too many of these at the same time and if I ever find myself in that place, then I need to plan better next time and set an intention to get better and better at this. As it happens, I am sweating a deadline right now. Not for this book, no. But I am helping a friend with her accounts and she's just been away on her holidays and her submission deadline is slightly less than four weeks away and I haven't been able to have a meeting with her yet since she got back from her holidays and her accountant is on my back. So this one isn't down to me, but I feel a sense of responsibility. This will get sorted because of those pressures. I wouldn't call it an emergency, but it is urgent. And did you notice all those "ands" I used in that sentence to describe it? That denotes a sort of breathlessness which is stress. Happily, we are over it now; we have it sorted and I can relax and re-focus.

Running out of money

Running out of money does feel like an emergency and one I have known for almost the entirety of my self-employed life. Sometimes life is on the up and money is plentiful. Sometimes the economic circumstances make life and business a lot tougher, cash dries up and I feel like I am on the way down. And most of the time I am somewhere in the middle. This sort of goes with the territory, it becomes your new normal, and I find it very reassuring to notice that much bigger businesses go through the same thing including, on the day I am writing this, Amazon, which is owned by a man who is currently regarded as one of the most successful in the world. So cut yourself some slack. This is business.

But here's the two things I have learned from my own businesses and those of my clients:

1. You don't die when you run out of money. So I wonder if that means it isn't an emergency then?

2. It always comes from somewhere. No matter how bleak and awful it feels, enough money to survive always comes from somewhere. So that would infer it's not an emergency either?

In my Small Business Big Magic group, which has been running for several years now, each of us take our turn in this place of feeling like we are running out of money and that it is an emergency. Usually it turns around fairly quickly. OK, it doesn't feel fast to you, my client, but that money always coming from somewhere usually turns up on average in our group within about three weeks. I don't speak to my client necessarily in that time and next time they drop in I think "Wow! That was quick!!" During that three weeks, your fallow period in the Fertile Void, your job is to do all you can from where you are with what you have and without panic. Give it a go. It gets easier, I promise. Oh, and remember to breathe.

Threats various

What other threats and emergencies are there? Tax bills and bills generally and letters from solicitors and government agencies tend to have threats attached to them, most of which never come to fruition and are just there to encourage you to respond in a timely fashion. Most things like that can be sorted out either with a calm review of the correspondence and reply thereto; often they go away entirely. Clean communication without panic is a good thing, and don't leave it right up against the deadline to reply because then your own options can be reduced or compromised due to shortage of time or time pressures. That's never a good way to do anything in my view.

If I were feeling poorly and I had things stacked up to do in my business which felt urgent I would try to work out what MUST I get done today without fail? Can I manage that? Yes = good. No = ask someone to help you or let the person who is waiting on you know the circumstances. Initially, they might be annoyed or disappointed, but they adjust very quickly so long as you don't make a habit of it. If you have no choice but to make a habit of it, then your emergency is your health (or the health of a loved one) and that must always be your #1 priority, good or bad, especially when you employ yourself for money. In those circumstances you might have some tough decisions to make, just for now until everyone's better again.

I think probably the best advice I can give you in an emergency is to slow down and think everything through. Usually, I let my clients talk and talk and talk until they are "empty". Sometimes we might do a Pros and Cons list before deciding. And we would end with "OK, what really needs to happen here?" When you are clear in your thoughts and feelings, that's usually obvious. If it isn't then you either haven't taken enough non-panicky time to review your options, or you haven't reached out to a friend, relative, or advice agency to get the help and support you need.

Do write and let me know which emergencies I haven't covered. I'm guessing that since you sent this question in ages ago, at the very start of my book-writing journey, you've survived your emergency again, in fact I know you have. Which tells me do you have an OS for emergencies.

NOTES

- **What's the most important thing that needs to happen here?**
- **Who's going to do it?**
- **Do I have all I need to get it done?**
- **Who will I ask for help?**

Question 45

WHEN IS IT OK TO BE BOTH A PERFECTIONIST AND A PROCRASTINATOR?

Never.

Next?

Only joking!

I hope my client takes this in good heart, as it is intended. Earlier this year she consulted me about opening a new business bank a/c. I gave her my advice as a woman who has been using business bank accounts for forty years. They are all the same. There is nothing to choose between them. They are not really interested in us despite what they say in their adverts. The banks are staffed by underpaid overworked clerks and I, for one, do not need an actual branch of a bank to go into and queue to make any form of transaction. I haven't banked a cheque since God was a lad, and if you are reading this in the UK, you should stop taking cheques immediately. Banks are anyway phasing them out, haven't you noticed?

My client wanted a bank which had online facilities with an App she liked. She decided upon HSBC where, as it happens, I do both my personal and business banking, and I too have the App though I mostly don't use it preferring to do my banking on my laptop for the bigger screen and the more grown-up interface. I can't bear it when they dumb it down which they mostly do on apps (gross generalisation, please forgive). But my client wanted the app because she is a woman who owns and uses a smartphone. She's out and about much more than I am and a busy woman likes to be able to do everything on the go, otherwise she would simply never get it all done. Busyness alert.

We discussed this across three (short) calls. But still… **three**, spread across perhaps ten days, maybe more. This is something I would have sorted myself on the afternoon it occurred to me I wanted to open a new bank account but, as I said, my client is a very busy woman, a businesswoman, a wife and mother. But, more relevant is the fact that she is both a professional and a perfectionist. Details are important to her, she wants to Get It Right. And no harm in that, provided you recognise the cost of the obsessing and you know when to **Stop It Immediately** and crack on.

And so, this led inevitably to my asking what on EARTH were the ongoing delays in this?

In the end, it came down to the fact that she was now reading the Ts and Cs before she signed the opening paperwork.

WTF?

WHO DOES THAT? What's the point anyway, because HSBC is not going to change their Ts and Cs for my client. Dream on! If she wants to open an account there, she has to sign it. End of.

We had a laugh, of course we did. Especially when I told her the story about the article I read recently about an organisation who set out to prove that no-one reads the Ts and Cs. They inserted a couple of funny clauses into theirs, one about giving up your first-born child to them, and the second one about doing thousands of hours of community service and everyone, to a man, signed the Ts and Cs without reading them. Except, I think, one person. And they gave that person a prize.

Save your energy for what's important. If you are a details person, all well and good. But choose to spend only the right amount of time on research, the appropriate amount of time for the task in hand, and no more. We are only opening a bank account here, not doing rocket science, addressing the G20 or doing something worthy of the Nobel Prize. Yet.

Here's another example of slowing yourself down and taking far too long to make up your mind because you are fearful of getting it wrong. It must be said that I have often not paid enough attention to some things like this, especially contracts. But my client and I would both be well served in moving toward each other's operating systems. Mine is fast and furious and hers is slow to stop. Mix 'em together and divide by two and you have your sweet spot.

NOTES

- **Is there something you are putting off because you are anxious you cannot do it perfectly?**
- **Do it today.**
- **How did it go?**

Question 46

WHY IS THERE SO MUCH WORK TO DO ALL THE TIME?

There's a deceptively large amount of work to be done by one person, isn't there?

Tell me about it!

I can't ever really remember being employed because it was so long ago but I do know that in a larger enterprise, everyone takes their part. But working for ourselves at home involves being all the departments. We are HR, legal, accounting, marketing, sales, warehousing, internal comms, transport, fulfilment, facilities management, IT and Uncle Tom Cobley.

I will confess that I don't need several of those departments in my own home-based biz but I do take care of HR (self-care), accounting (natch), marketing, sales, and fulfilment (doing the "real" work). I almost never have a need for legal. I once used a solicitor when I sold my first business but I wouldn't worry about things going wrong unless they do. Depending on what you do, most of it isn't terribly legally risky, unless you teach people to jump out of planes without a parachute, I guess. Or the equivalent.

And I am geeky and mostly run my own tech, but I do have a wonderful chap I can turn to in extremis and he's worth his weight in gold.

If you are a one-man or one-woman band, there is a lot to do. So we'd better crack on then! Always remembering you do not have to do it all unless, again, that is your choice.

I am imagining that perhaps you might wonder about how to afford all the help you need - lawyer, accountant, computer support, outsourcing etc. And only you can decide what you will make important and what you will find the money to pay for to free you up to do what you are good at. But if you are going to learn to do and master everything, you are going to need more than 24 hours in a day. And to give up sleeping.

This is one of the reasons why I recommend what I call One Woman One Website, i.e. one central project. Because if you run multiple projects you have to do all those jobs in all those projects. IMPOSSIBLE.

In my own work, I pretty much confine myself to wearing two hats. Marketing/Sales, and fulfilment (being with my clients). I do the former so that I can do the latter.

My computer mostly doesn't go wrong. One careful lady owner.

I do my own accounts once a month on either the last day of this or the first day of next.

And I'm quite geeky when it comes to my own website etc. But if you are not, get help.

If you need help deciding what to pay someone else to do for you, and how you are going to fund that, come and ask.

I would advise the following strategies:

- Keep everything as simple as possible, streamline it all, remember there is just one woman doing all of this, so do only what needs to be done and give up perfectionism. Again.

- Work out what's really important, and that's top-notch customer and client service, focus on your clients.

- At our level, you must master marketing and sales, I can teach you that, it isn't hard, honest.

- Everything else can be bought in.

- Don't try to do everything and, if you do want to learn it all, don't try to learn it all at once or feel proficient in all of it before you offer yourself to your paying public. You can learn as you go. I am still learning.

- Do all you can to avoid overwhelm. Work out a simple plan that looks like it might work for you. Then simplify that plan still further.

I know from my diary what I am scheduled to do today, this week and this month. That's enough for me to have a feel of the shape of those different chunks of time. I know that they are taking me in a generally forward direction in every sense, and I know when I can squeeze in chunks of time for learning new things I want to master.

Breathe. And take care of you first, above all else. Relax! You've got this.

- **What tasks in your business must be done by you and you alone? Clue: not as many as you think!**

- Eventually what sort of help would you like to find to take care of the rest?
- What plan do you have, for now, for getting everything done that needs doing, and no more?

Question 47

WHY DO I NOT HAVE CONTROL OF MY OWN DAY?

"I've no boss and just the normal domestic roles (plus a few voluntary bits) but I still seem to lose way too many days to other people's drama."

The short answer is I have no idea. If we were speaking in one of my coaching calls I'd be able to ask you a few more clarifying questions. Given we don't have that luxury today, I'm going to hazard a few guesses and hope that one at least is on the money.

Firstly, when you say you have "just the normal domestic roles (plus a few voluntary bits)" that already denotes a busy woman to me. And perhaps the way in which you operate in both those areas of your life are hangovers from the days before you started to employ yourself for money?

I don't have any normal domestic roles. I am gloriously unrepentantly single and that gives me total and 100% freedom to direct my energies and spend my time on working with my clients, marketing my business and writing this book. There are no distractions except those I allow or seek out. I run My Biz My Way and you can too.

I think you probably tend to underestimate how challenging and time-consuming "normal domestic roles" can be. I always wonder on holiday how on earth I have time to work too when I am at home. By the time I've got myself up and showered, we've had breakfast, done the shopping, washed the clothes, had some fun and a trip out and made the meals, when would one work in that? That's only "normal domestic" stuff and you've added "a few voluntary bits on top". I don't have those either. Those are your choice, I've made mine. Priority first, then focus next. Only you can decide what you will chop/streamline, and what you will keep. But you are going to need to make some room for that new biz or creative pursuit of yours.

One thing that might be useful is to think that if you had a day job, you'd need to fit in all the activities in those roles around your 35-40 hours a week away from home at your workplace and after commuting too. Most people in jobs do the stuff you are talking about in evenings and weekends. Do you? Do you have that discipline? The idea is to ring-fence the time you choose to spend working on your own business so that you are off limits to everyone and everything else during those vital hours. This constitutes nothing more than taking yourself seriously as a businesswoman and creator, denoting self-respect and self-esteem.

One of the best things about being self-employed, in Judith world at least, is that you DON'T have to do those things rammed into evenings and weekends when everyone else is doing it. You can see daylight and do these things during the off-peak weekdays. But know that if you do that, you either have to work at your self-employed stuff in evenings/weekends instead, as I do, or you have simply stolen from yourself the time and energy it takes to run Your Biz Your Way, unless this is your way of course but it doesn't seem like it is because your question has a slightly resentful tone to it, as though you don't yet understand your own behaviour and why you allow other people (OP) to play fast and loose with you and your days.

I suspect also that you are simply a Nice Girl. You are just a girl who can't say no to other people's requests of you and that may be your kids, your partner, your aging parents, your next-door neighbour, your dog, or whomsoever asks. You must keep your kids alive (and a bit more TBH), you have to do your bit in a relationship to keep that alive too and, with parents, this is also important. You may be at that stage of life where you are juggling all three. What can you do in Your Biz around those commitments? What will you prioritise and what will you shelve, for now, in order to get back control of your day? What do you need to be able to learn to do and say?

Everything is a choice, even the stuff that doesn't feel like it very much. I worked with my own coach, the very wonderful Michael Neill, for a year way back in 2006 and a major focus of our work together FOR A YEAR (did I say that??) was to stop me being so darned **dutiful**, specifically to get me out of a 2-day a week commitment to one of my former accounting clients. I resigned on 5th September 2006 in the end, and left (ha ha) on 28th February 2007. It is so easy to feel that you have got "stuck" doing stuff for other people simply because you always have and cannot see an easy way out, especially stuff you love for people you love, as I did in this example.

What would you say no to, if you could, in order to get that control back? And, I don't really like the word control TBH. I wonder if there's another word we could choose that would be more helpful, I'm thinking about choices and allowing, rather than feeling you have to control things or be controlled. Very restrictive, control; it feels heavy and onerous.

You give me a big clue with the "other people's drama" piece. Well, in a nutshell, that's it, isn't it? You are allowing those dramas to be more important than your business and your day, and you end up feeling frustrated by the losses to you. How much longer are you going to go on doing that? What do you think would help?

Sorry to use a coachy jargony word (by now you'll appreciate how much I dislike those) which trips so easily off the tongue, especially when I know you know this already, but this is a boundaries thing, isn't it? It's about learning to say no, or no, not now. We often don't know how to do that, or to do it in a way that is fair. It may be simply a matter of not picking up the requests, or not over-responding, or very quickly assessing the situation and saying I can't help you with that, but X might. Or I'm at work now, I can't do this for you today, but I could take an hour out over the weekend, or your own variations of those as appropriate to the request.

I would even go so far as to go overboard with this initially, repel all boarders. Be strict. Blame me. Say I'm not getting enough done in my business/my creative endeavours and my coach says (fill in the blanks). Increasingly show others how they can help themselves, empower them as opposed to allowing them to steal your most precious resources whether or not they know that's what they are doing.

Just say no.

You might find it useful, while you have your training wheels on, to rehearse a few of these reasons why you cannot be interrupted/help now, and type them up and have them right next to you and work your way through a rotating list of them, until you feel able to respond in the moment. Another useful tip is to say "I'm not sure. I need to look at my diary. Can I get back to you by close of business Friday?" or some such. Give yourself a breathing space in which to respond, not over-respond or react. Give yourself that time to work out if you want to do it at all these days, or whether you just do it because you always have; no need to be a martyr all your life! Give yourself that time to work out how you are going to fit it in around your business, or if your lovely little biz and your day will be the losers again.

I have often found it is useful to set up things in a way which suits a Nice Girl e.g. by letting everyone know that you will be focusing on your biz between the hours of X and Y (your choice) and that during that time you will not be answering either personal emails or phone calls or interruptions of any description unless they come from loved ones who are mortally wounded or unless the house is on fire. Make it funny!

Simply not being available 24/7 to other people changes everything. You start to put yourself first and take your biz seriously. You start to put yourself first for a change. If you want this to change, you must learn to put yourself first.

The best way to achieve this, after your initial announcement, is by your actions not by your words. People won't believe your words. You've always been available to them on demand and until you stop being that over-responsive nice girl/mum/dutiful daughter/artist/accountant, they will always continue to expect it and to feel it is more than OK to put upon you. Again. Historically you've been complicit in this, but no more!

My experience is that non-family people who put upon you in this way simply move off once you stop meeting their needs emotional and practical. Remember my saying they are what I call successful people? They are successful at getting their own needs met first and foremost, often at the expense of others and, at the moment, that's at your expense in every way. Those people have been my nemesis too, more than once. They will respond to your new non-availability by simply shuffling off and finding someone else to meet their needs. It's like this drinking hole has run dry, so they move on in search of another one they can bleed dry too. Can you bleed dry a drinking hole? No, probably not, just a human being, just a Nice Girl.

You get control of your day by setting your intentions, creating new habits of discipline and self-discipline, allowing fewer and fewer interruptions except when it is a matter of life or death, and acting like a woman who has some boundaries until you wake up one day and discover that you have become that woman. And when that day comes, this will cease to be a problem for you. Life becomes much calmer. You realise and appreciate precisely how much choice you really do have over everything and everyone in your life, including and especially yourself.

Decide what's important to you and only let distractions get in the way of your business which you consider to be equally or more important than your business, and prioritise accordingly. Make a list of those things now. I would start with your health (emotional and otherwise) and the health and well-being of those you love. After those two, everything's up for grabs. Everything's negotiable. Everything's a choice.

You don't have to - unless you want to - do this in a Wham Bam Thankyou Mam BIG ANNOUNCEMENT way. Or even today. You can do it slow and steady in a way that builds. So you don't need to turn into the Wicked Witch of the West right this red hot second so that they think you're having a breakdown. But slowly and surely you increasingly stand firm to your principles and everything changes, inch by inch.

You might start training yourself by saying such things as "come hell or high water, I am going to get X done today." And if you find that you get to bedtime and you haven't done it, either you stay up until you have, punishing yourself in a way that will soon become tiresome, or you accept that tomorrow is another day and that you were a wuss who let the world get the better of her AGAIN. Forgive yourself if that's it, and have another go tomorrow and tomorrow and tomorrow. You'll crack this in the end.

Now, some balance… some days we eat the bear, some days the bear eats us. But we want more of the former. A lot more of the former.

Over to you! Let me know how it goes and if I can help some more.

NOTES

- **Who is your main bugbear when it comes to this?**
- **How could you start to change that dynamic today?**
- **What will you do differently so they get the message loud and clear? Don't overdo it! One day at a time. Don't burn your boats unless that's the only option and you are overdue for a bonfire.**

Question 48

HOW DO WE RESPOND TO UNFAIR ONLINE REVIEWS?

"I think my main 'issue' is that we are judged on the Internet with reviews - sometimes fairly and sometimes (it feels) unfairly, irrelevant, off topic, bizarre

and totally randomly. We know we can't please all of the people etc., but how to stick to cancellation Ts & Cs when someone you know WILL write you a bad review because they feel it's not fair you have charged them even though it was the contract they signed up to."

I would find this very difficult myself, not being a fan very much of feedback or criticism or misunderstandings and, funnily enough, I am helping some people this morning with something similar, you know… you said, I said, your side, our side etc.

I think in your industry the fault lies with the tyranny of those online booking sites and how inflated a sense of their own importance they have and the damaging aspects of even just one bad review which is really only opinion when it comes right down to it. And with opinions, we all have different ones all of the time. I really feel for you when that happens, as of course it always will in your type of biz.

Is that why an industry expert of our mutual acquaintance encourages owners to build up repeat bookings and direct relationships? Yet even there there's the potential for things to go wrong. We cannot please all of the people all of the time, as you say, and that's hard on us sensitive types who want it all to be lovely for everyone 24/7 and in perpetuity.

I suppose we have to build up a business-like response and park it in a box marked 9-5 (my new thing). Behaviour and cultural expectations go both ways, don't they? This is a sticky one, as stuff between people always has the potential to be.

What it reminds me of is when someone gets sacked or leaves a job. And when a relationship ends. Those of us on the sacked/chucked side feel sad and misunderstood. But I think most onlookers who have a fair grasp of the situation from both sides can see it in the round and take their own balanced view.

So it is with reviews. I think some people reading them will see the truth, however the story is told. If all your other reviews are excellent, which I know they are, then anyone you would want to stay with you can take the reviews as a whole and factor that in. One bad review doesn't make you bad. Most of us know how difficult people can be and often that is very transparent in a review if the reviewer comes across as a weirdo.

I am not much of a one for reading or writing reviews. I just see your place and want to stay there and I forget often to consider what other people thought. But I know you feel bad when it drags your overall rating down for a while and how much work goes into that climbing slowly back up due to the weighting of bad reviews.

I don't have an answer for this one. It just goes with the territory and in time you will become just more accepting of their rough with your smooth.

When I sold my accountancy business it was because their rough had started to rob me of my smooth.

And there have been times in my coaching business when I have attracted difficult and/or disruptive clients, but not right now I notice and I can only think that's because of me, the vibe I put out, the comfort I have in my own self and, as you say, knowing I cannot help everyone either and nor should I try. So, weirdly, those people have stopped showing up in my reality.

I work with clients enough to know that into each of their lives from time to time a little rain must fall. Or a mahoosive great thunderstorm. Since you are a diligent member of SBBM you have also seen these rain showers and even torrents occasionally. But they pass. They pass. And with their passing so do our feelings of sadness, leaving us just a little bit more steely and businesslike. I know this to be true because we have more recently discussed another one of these, and you'd already composed the perfect reply and found your equilibrium before we even talked. And you did it fast.

For as long as you are reasonably happy to continue to run the business that you have, this is going to be a small and diminishing part of it. People are weird, some guests even weirder. But the more you can park this in the box marked 9-5 and perhaps even tap on the feelings so that they feel less and less unfair to you if they even feature at all, then how you feel about this aspect of your biz will change in a way which will feel better and better to you. And given that we can't change the others, that's all I care about.

NOTES

- Do you use the review sections of websites before you buy? Historically I have always forgotten to do that myself.
- But, now that we know how important it is to other small business owners just like us, will we remember to leave more good reviews, the sort we'd want to receive for our businesses? Appreciative, cheerleading and real? Useful for our peers, useful for their customers.
- Look how it could perk up a business who'd been on the receiving end of an awful and unfair online review, and what a difference we could make to that one. We can be the difference we want to see in the world.

Question 49

HOW DO I DECIDE WHETHER AND WHEN TO EXPAND?

"I am freelance and have been for 20 years but I wonder if you have any advice about knowing when to stick with freelance or move to expand, possibly using associates. I really like the freedom of being freelance but I sometimes wonder if I am leveraging my skill set enough."

This is a fascinating conundrum.

I've been freelance, self-employed, a business owner, a director of a limited company, and a partner in a business. I think I have tried on every variety of working for myself that exists. Mostly, they aren't better, they are just different.

No, I lie. Today the one I like best is just being me.

However, let's take yours at face value, starting with the point you make at the end.

You wonder if you are leveraging your skill set enough. OK, only you can decide this, always remembering that there's no requirement to do **everything** of which we are capable.

For instance, people say I would have made a great mother. I'm not so sure myself. But either way, I didn't go that route.

I was an excellent county-level swimmer. I might have trained for something superhuman like say crossing the English Channel to France. But I did not.

Did I have the capacity for either of those in me? Probably. Do I care that I haven't done either of them and explored my possibilities to the max? No.

So that's what I mean by only you can decide. There's no requirement to do that. And it will be different and bring new challenges, which you might like more or even less.

You say you like the freedom of being freelance. Quite. I do too. It is strangely addictive knowing that you don't have to take any or all the work that comes to you, knowing that it is always your choice is very liberating. But what about if you had other mouths to feed in your biz, as it were? Would it feel so good or would there be compromises involved?

The reasons for expanding, possibly using associates, would be to make more money for less personal effort in delivery. But you might need to work just as hard in other directions. Finding work to feed those associates, as inferred above. So is that work you would relish for a change? Building your brand, taking on and managing projects, taking on and managing and training associates?

Managing. Managing. Managing. I've done that and I didn't like it as much.

Could you experiment and see? I don't think there's a knowing in advance, except in your gut. My knowing came from doing and I didn't like it as much as being on my own and when I work with clients who have staff and associates, there's a lot of frustration which goes along with that.

That in itself is not a reason not to experiment.

How about a pros and cons list, for starters? You are quite process-orientated, I know that about you. Draw up reasons for doing it and against doing it and measure them.

I think probably the main reason for doing it would be because your desire for change and challenge outweighs how much you enjoy your freedom. I think you must be experiencing a sense of that otherwise I don't think the question would have occurred to you to ask at all. Am I right?

NOTES

- **What are the joys of working in the way you currently do?**
- **And the restrictions?**
- **On a scale of 1-10, how ready are you for a change or a challenge?**

Question 50

HOW MUCH TIME SHOULD I PUT INTO A NEW AREA OF BUSINESS OUTSIDE MY SWEET SPOT?

"How to discern how much time to put into a new area of business (outside one's sweet spot) that could be of real benefit further down the road e.g. training work flows to me but I am interested in building up my list to generate more affiliate income but right now I find the creation of videos a bit tedious because I am still making a lot of mistakes."

How long is a piece of string? I know you to be a wise bird, and vice versa, and were this me I would put in as much time as I was able to find the passion or interest or enthusiasm for and I note that you use the word interest so this doesn't sound as though it would be hard for you.

What's the real problem?

Are you wiped out after completing your other work/family commitments?

I notice you mention videos and that you are finding that a bit tedious. If so, I wouldn't be building my list like that then. Although I briefly flirted with the idea of video yesterday (hush my mouth), you know I HATE video. But if anything is tedious I wouldn't do it. The beauty of self-employment is that a job that tedious doesn't occur or is simply outsourced, unless you are wedded to doing it the hard way.

How could this be easy, given that video isn't the only way? Or have you decided that it would be the best or fastest way, I wonder? In which case, persevere. But on your own head be it.

The best and fastest way for me would be to do something I love so much I couldn't stop myself doing it.

I've made a long list of the ways I intend to market this book, for instance, and all of them are things I would find fun, or interesting, even the slightly challenging-looking ones. But there are definitely no tedious ones on that list. Tedious? *Non merci.* Not much video on the list either! Did you go on a course which said video was The Way to do this list-building lark?

So here's another thought. If affiliate income is your goal, you don't necessarily need a list to do that anymore. There are other ways. And there are even early hints that email marketing is dead or dying. Wouldn't that be a bummer, to spend years building up a list only to discover (as I think I already have) that almost no-one bothers with emails anymore?

Right now, you and I are having a lot of fun on Facebook. Do you have a Facebook Page for this particular project? If you build an engaged following there, you could achieve your goals without a list at all. I am on a course this very week teaching me how to make the best of my Facebook Page and intend to get more into that so we can compare notes.

These days I tend to regard Facebook Pages and Groups as lists by another name.

I think what I am saying is twofold:

1. Don't do anything tedious, do something you'd love or at least prefer instead then it doesn't become a matter of how much time so much as "let me at it!"

2. There's more than one way, there are always many ways to achieve our end goal. How else could you create a reliable affiliate income which, by the way, I think is a good idea for you, you Mechanic* you?

NOTES

- **If something's proving tedious, what's the message?**
- **What other ways could you achieve your goal which you WOULD enjoy?**
- **Remember what I always say: "When it's right, it's easy!"**

Question 51

WHY AM I WAKING IN THE NIGHT WITH REMORSE AND TERRORS?

"The overarching optimism of a new idea that makes anything possible during

the day, followed by the 4:00 a.m. sudden waking to remorse and terrors, depending how far I've got embroiled in the idea."

Wow! Been there, done that, got the T-shirt.

I don't know that I wake at 4 a.m. with remorse and terrors except if I have bitten off more than I can chew. Which isn't necessarily a reason to stop the idea in its tracks, unless you decide that it is. Or maybe this is just your psyche keeping you safe for good reasons, or for small fearful reasons.

I am more likely to wake at 4 a.m. or stay awake all night if I am excited about a new idea or project which I really know is The One, or The One For Now Or For Next. And another way I know it is if I would prefer to work on it today than all the other lovely things in my diary, if I can't wait to get to it.

Given how many ideas-related questions you have provided me with for this book, for which endless thanks by the way, I think when you do get the nameless dreads in the middle of the night they are probably a sign to stop or slow down and do more evaluation before you rush headlong into another brilliant idea, 'cos all our ideas are brilliant, right? All mine are anyway!

What's happened to me over the years since I've discovered I am a Creator* with a propensity to be a Scanner is that I've learned to manage myself, to master myself if you will. I used to have a go at all of my ideas or most of them, and that was the way I discovered I had to focus on far fewer, ideally just The One.

It didn't mean I stopped being creative or having ideas. Far from it. But I trained myself to either record or abandon all the irrelevant ones, and use the good ones for the benefit of my main project instead.

So in my coaching work, I corral all my ideas into my marketing, into writing this book, and into working with my clients, not necessarily in that order. And they all combine to make up The One. And that way I feel totally fulfilled in fully expressing all my creativity.

But in the last fifteen years or so I've had all sorts of brilliant ideas and put all of them into action, some of them more than one at once, and all that happened was that everything failed or was compromised, or I exhausted myself, or both.

These days I find that smaller ideas, or smaller bits of bigger ideas, are of more use to me and my clients and my One Thing.

I remain an optimist. I even love the alliteration of being an overarching one. What I would encourage you to do, Gentle Reader, is feel into the remorse and the terrors to find the messages that lie therein. If you are not sure, carry on and see if the mists clear or if it gets foggier still. I don't think ideas are scary in and of themselves. Just what we attach to them.

NOTES

- **What wakes you in the night?**
- **What do you do then?**
- **Abundant Rachael Greenland taught me that when you can't sleep, the next best thing is to lie there with your eyes closed, resting. And to take the pressure off yourself and your anxiety about sleeplessness. Try it. It works. Remind yourself as you do it that Judith and Rachael say this is nearly as good as sleep. And so it is.**

Question 52

WHY CAN'T I SUFFER FOOLS GLADLY?

"Not suffering fools gladly - the dreadful realisation that even if I was offered a conventional job, my dislike of being told what to do by someone I don't respect wouldn't be pretty."

I don't see the problem here. Surely this is precisely the reason we are self-employed, so we don't have to?

Crack on! There are an awful lot of fools out there, you are right. And the good news is they are not in here. Well, most days they are not in here where the only numpty is, on occasion, *moi*!

BREATHING SPACE – CHAPTER SEVEN- PRACTICAL

Chapter Seven discusses how to spot emergencies, the twin perils of perfectionism and procrastination, getting it all done and/or under control, unfairness, expansion, tedium, remorse, terrors and suffering! Sounds like a bit of a grim chapter, eh? But I hope you found something useful in there for you.

How often do emergencies happen to you, and are you OK with that?

Have you conquered all the various dreads that my lovely questioners have brought up for the benefit of all of us?

Can you feel yourself becoming just a little more steely when required, and devil-may-care when not?

Do you trust yourself enough to decide when to expand, contract, control, allow, do something that isn't tedious, and recognise remorse and terrors and suffering for what they really are? Good! You are getting the hang of this then. Told you.

So here's your last breathing space in which you can write down whatever thoughts come to mind. Things you will let go, and those you will keep. Those things you want to celebrate and those you will change. How about some lovely intentions for the next year? My intention is to make this book an annual thing, because I know questions will always arise. I am happy for you to pop into Ask Judith at any time and check that the decision you have taken about having your biz your way is the right one for you. And to remind you that if it turns out not to be, in any small or big way, you can simply either change your mind or **Stop It Immediately!**

So how about using this space for exactly that?
What do you choose to change your mind about?
And what will you **stop immediately?**
What else comes to mind?

_____

_____

_____

_____

_____

_____

_____

_____

_____

_____

_____

CHAPTER EIGHT

Judith

(the Questions I Wish You'd Asked, but Didn't!)

THE IMPORTANCE OF BEING ABLE TO CHANGE YOUR MIND

Knowing that I can change my mind about anything, and do it in this exact moment, is possibly the single most valuable thing I have learned about myself in life and in business. And consequently I have reminded you often about that in these pages.

The older I am, the less certain I am about anything and everything. And as you get older too you may come to understand this, assuming you do not already.

Sometimes when friends, clients and colleagues are telling me things they believe which make them miserable or suffer in any way, I offer them the opportunity to change their mind. They don't like it. It makes them cross. And I'm not surprised. Some of the things we think we believe we cling to very tightly. We erroneously believe they are facts. We have always considered our unexamined worldview to be The Truth.

But mostly you can just change your mind about anything.

Let me give you an example.

I am advising a business at the moment where they are moving from one reality of the world and of their business to another which is diametrically opposed to the way they used to do it. It is very unsettling for the 3-person team, some more than others. The ones who have been able to move more easily with it are the least stuck in their ways/the most flexible in their thinking. If you are somewhat old-fashioned, as I am in some things, values mostly, then it can be difficult to change. If you have always been taught to believe that something must be a certain way, then you tend to believe that is the only way. It isn't.

Clinging to the old ways which are your safety blanket, when everything around you is shifting, feels entirely logical. But it is your clinging which is misery-making.

You could just change your mind. It really is that simple. Your thoughts about the facts are making you miserable, not the facts themselves. Everything changes all the time. Nothing stays the same. And changing your mind about anything is liberating and empowering. Once you get used to it, it feels good.

Now, I am not recommending here that you become rudderless, adrift on a hostile sea, drifting around and feeling lost and scared. Instead, I think you must consider if you could adapt to thinking of the changes as new adventures, and think of them as keeping you flexible and young, and of yourself as a person who can shift quickly with life's changes when it is called for. We can also decide or remember to trust, as I've said over and over in this book, that the Big U has our back.

We don't always know the answers to stuff. But generally, they do show up if we abide in trust the meanwhile. And they are more likely to do that if we are not stuck in our ways and wedded to the solution being our way or something we feel we must create or control.

Roll with it. And STAND YOUR GROUND when none of this applies. LOL! See me if you are not sure which is which.

ONE DAY AT A TIME: TRAINING YOUR SELF-EMPLOYED MUSCLE

One of my newer clients is struggling to meet his weekly commitments to himself in his business. He's relatively new to this self-employment lark. He booked three appointments with me at weekly intervals, to help him get off the starting block. He blew me out for the first one because he hadn't got as much done as he wanted and, I'm guessing, he didn't want to show up and tell me that.

So on Tuesday of the next week I PM'd him via Facebook and asked about progress so that he still had three days to get his act together before we were due to speak next. I was quite determined on his behalf that he would achieve more this week.

Here's how our exchange went:

Me: Hi, just thought I'd give you a nudge in case one was needed.
Him: Hi Judith, Thanks for the nudge. I have been still somewhat battling against myself. However, I am more focused today and methodically tackling tasks. I hope that I will be able to carry this momentum forward into tomorrow and so on. I look forward to catching up on Friday. At this present moment, I feel like my first goal must be to get some kind of momentum back. If by Friday I can have accomplished that alone I will consider it a victory. I am sorry not to be able to report bigger strides, but I am still determined to get back up on my feet.
Me: It's OK. I know what it's like. Do you want to send me a PM at the end of today, tomorrow and Thursday like accountability training wheels? Up to you entirely.
Him: Yes, that would be great. I'll PM you this evening with tomorrow's tasks/plan. I think just focusing one day at a time might be the surest way forward for now.

Later he did precisely that, sent me a list of things he intended to take care of today, Wednesday. And I replied:

Me: It will be good to get better at estimating what you can get done in a day and working out the extent of your determination to finish a list, however wrong you get the length of the lists to begin with. I think I pretty much know what I can get done in a day and when I've done enough I stop, and when I've been a bit flaky I push through until it's all done but that's after DECADES of training myself! But that's all I believe this is... training ourselves to be efficiently and effectively self-employed. Thanks, by the

> *way, I think I can get something out of this for my book! Good luck with your Wednesday.*
>
> Him: *Yes, I definitely need to work on an understanding of how much I can get done in a day. Also rebuilding my will to push through when it gets choppy. I'll send you a message this time tomorrow.*

So, you can see there are people and strategies that can help you, whatever the problem is that you are coping with alone today. If not me, then find an accountability partner, another self-employed person who, when left alone to their own devices at home, finds it just as difficult as you to focus and Get Stuff Done. You are both entirely normal in this regard, not bonkers at all. No sooner had I set up this daily mini-reporting with this particular client than another joined in too with her version.

In 2017 the distractions are many and varied. Even while writing this today I've been downstairs to the kitchen for breakfast, looked inside the dishwasher, thought about unloading it, come back upstairs with coffee and messed about tidying up my desktop (!) and printing out podcast crib sheets and marking them up with episode numbers, recording dates and air dates when I won't be using them for more than a month yet. And mucked about on Facebook a bit, replied to a couple of emails to keep my inbox at zero which is how I like it best. And I am one of the most focused and efficient people I know!

You really don't know what procrastination is until you start to employ yourself for money, or write a book. Distractions abound.

But the good news is that you can be trained, rather like you were in a job. And this time you get to decide the training schedule, namely what sort of self-employed muscles you want, and you notice yourself getting stronger day by day at something you just resolve to continue to apply yourself. Every day in every way you are getting better and better. But you won't unless you keep making a little incremental progress every day. That's the name of this game.

I was laughing with a friend earlier today (oops, forgot to list that in my distractions) about how I'd had to bribe myself through a couple of tasks I was doing for her recently on her accounts. No coffee till I've done October. No watching Suits until I've done November and December. Those were my two fave bribes during August. Soon they will change, as I do, but the principle will remain. Honestly, People, whatever it takes to get the job done. Whatever it takes.

Employing yourself for money isn't all fun and larks. It mostly is, in as much as no two days are the same and we can organise things so that we don't have to do too much of what we dislike. But we won't amount to a hill of beans unless and until we can find some self-discipline and that can be trained into us, and a buddy can help.

A couple of weeks after I wrote this, my client and I postponed his third call because, again, he wasn't making as much progress as fast as he hoped. BUT - and get this - he wrote last night to say:

"Hi Judith, just a quick message to let you know that I've had an excellent day! I got up at five and have been working on #1. It has basically taken me the whole day to produce a 15-minute video but that has included writing a script, building a makeshift sound studio at my desk, learning to use ScreenFlow, recording audio and screen separately, editing... and more. I've learned a huge amount. Tomorrow I'm going to aim to complete #2. Haven't felt this fired up in months... or maybe years."

Woo Hoo! Woo Hoo! Woo Hoo! You see? We get there in the end. From zero to hero in three weeks.

What did I tell you about three weeks? Three weeks has a magic all its own.

WHAT ARE YOU REALLY WORTH?

A lot of clients turn up in my life asking me to help them evaluate their business model. What they really want to know is "Does it add up?" And even if they don't want to know that, I do.

I can only understand the value of what on earth you are up to when I can see how much money you are going to make from your efforts, and how easily.

There's another sort of client who turns up too, one who's already discovered that they are working far too hard for scant return. It's not working, or it feels like it's not.

So, depending on what you do, I need to be able to see how many of your things you have to sell in order to make the money you want and deserve for your expertise or talent, and for your long years of blood sweat and tears to get to this place in your life and work. And I mostly want you to take the short route too.

These assessments go approximately the same way.

1. What's your financial target? What do you need/want to earn from your business?

2. How many units do you need to sell each month/year to make that?

3. If your service or product fixes people easily, in one to three sessions, does that mean you are going to be constantly marketing forever to get the high turnover or clients to make that target? I know first-hand how taxing this can be, and I love it, but it's time-consuming and it will be especially difficult for you if you don't really like marketing or sales or find them icky. It isn't really a good business model either, it's a labour of love.

4. Is there another, better way?

5. What are you **really** worth?

Typically what we all do is work too hard for too little. That's where we start. Then it either starts to hurt you or I point out this isn't great. It might work for a bit, but it isn't sustainable. I did it like that, to some extent, during my time as an accountant or certainly in the early years anyway. My clients break down far sooner.

Often the reason the newly self-employed get into this weird and broken place is that you've never directly asked clients and customers for money before, and you erroneously assume people won't want to pay you very much. Typically (but not exclusively) people who don't pay you very much are quite demanding, and you end up doing just as much work for someone who pays you £100 as you do for someone who pays you £1,000, often more (unbelievably!).

Now, that may seem like a big jump. But the truly amazing thing is that someone who pays you £1,000 is just all round a much easier client to have. They comprehend the relationship between time and money. They respect your expertise. They don't fuss and fret over every detail, leaving you to do what you are good at. They know how to make decisions, and quickly without keeping you waiting. They trust and value you and your expertise, what I call your "cred". They know how to be a good client because they've already learned this lesson for themselves and they are totally at peace and ease with it. They know what expertise costs and, more importantly, they appreciate its value.

With clients who pay you what you are truly worth, your business just starts to go much more smoothly and you can afford all the help you need as well, making life much easier.

Now, I know what you're thinking… I feel this too. **"BUT I WANT TO HELP THE LITTLE PEOPLE!"** Yes, I know you do. We all do.

But - and this I promise - if you will just put the oxygen mask on yourself first and make yourself and your own business strong by charging what you are really worth, then you can give away as much as you like later on and help all the little people from that place of strength. You cannot do that from a place of scarcity and exhaustion, only from a place of abundance and surplus.

Your natural inclinations are good, but you cannot start there, not unless you are Mother Theresa.

Here's the kicker. All those little people you want to help? They are being targeted by every other business out there just like ours and they can't afford to work with any one of us, let alone all of us. So, put the tiddlers back.

Take it first to those who can easily afford you, and then later you can give it away all you like.

GOOD, GOOD, GOOD VIBRATIONS

For some of my clients, that's who I am. The woman who once a month, or more often, helps to raise their vibration when they have fallen into a slump. I really like to be used like this, as a cheerleader. Clients call me the Queen of Positive Thinking. Maybe. Certainly my bestie says, in jest I think, that I live in La La Land (not the musical, the name of my favourite Jessica nail polish!). I'll confess it is always easy for me to see the upside, especially about you, because you are so gorgeous in every way.

Working alone at home, or even at the office if your business has one, can be a lonely business especially if you are at the top of the tree, making all the decisions and having the buck stop with you.

Mud sticks. And too much mud starts to weigh you down horribly. And without the perspective of a team at your level with whom to share the burdens, or a water-cooler moment or a group laugh or hug, you get low. I know you do.

So, in that instance, my job is to raise your vibe. Please do not underestimate how important it is to be radiating the good ones. Yes, I'll always be here doing that. But imagine you could get yourself into that place every morning or in any moment when life feels a bit pants.

How would you do that? Answers on a postcard please. Meanwhile here are some clues to get you going:

- Laughter
- Music and singing along and dancing too if the fancy takes you. Like nobody's watching. Nobody is.
- Physical exercise, a walk, a run, a swim, the thing you know that always makes you feel better when you do it
- Reading something uplifting, realising you are not alone and not the only person to have faced adversity

- Looking up from your desk or from your laptop and looking at life/the problem from a different perspective
- Counting your blessings
- A walk in nature
- Playing with your pets
- Doing one thing at a time
- Meditating
- Diverting yourself from what you consider to be the problem giving it room to magically shift
- Trusting that solutions can arrive without you necessarily having to fix everything all of the time
- Hobbies - doing things you love for no good reason. I'm thinking of taking up jewellery-making, jigsaw puzzling, and returning to colouring-in. No apologies. The heart wants what the heart wants, remember?
- Taking a duvet day or even just a nap. I find a nap can be a bit of a cure-all, ditto a good night's sleep
- Hanging out with those you love
- Reminding yourself it's only work and worse things happen at sea
- Calling me
- Emailing me
- PMing me
- Enjoying and sharing social media but only if it raises you up; steer well clear if it brings you down
- Writing down three unique things for which you are grateful; it works, do it every day. We have so much to be grateful for
- Going onto YouTube and tapping along with Brad Yates (EFT) with a view to releasing today's unhelpful emotion
- Watching a funny cat video or a soppy dog one or some small furry animals (one's enough!)
- Going for a drive

- Cooking something nourishing and delicious for yourself and your family for tonight. I always get a lovely feeling from stirring the pot, knowing that I love myself enough to have made myself a delicious and nourishing supper for later, or lunch for now.
- Phoning a friend (not my bag, in the main, but fill yer boots!)
- Volunteering
- Checking your reality with someone who can get you to see perspective and to stop taking it all so seriously
- Picking something off your self-care list and doing it
- Going for a massage or a manicure
- Putting on your wellies and stomping through puddles in the rain or scuffing through piles of crunchy autumn leaves
- Getting a haircut (did that today)
- Stepping away from the machine
- Finding a philosophical place of acceptance with whatever is going on

What's your favourite way of raising your vibration? I do hope you'll find a way to let me know.

DO YOU WANT TO LEAVE A LEGACY?

I don't have any sense that I want to leave a legacy when I shuffle off this mortal coil. I am very content to make my difference in this lifetime.

But lots of my clients do want to leave a legacy. And, if you do, good on you.

And if you are more like me, just know this isn't compulsory. Leaving a legacy is not a requirement of self-employment, or of life.

Do I think it's a bad thing? Certainly not. It just isn't something I feel personally. And if there's a message at all in this book it is to be your own person and to stop blindly following others and being like those you admire. Just be you. It's enough. It's more than enough.

Legacy can be created through our work, for sure. There's a woman called Judith Morgan, who isn't me. Well, there are a few of them, but the one I am telling you about today is dead. I have a Google alert set on my own name so that I can monitor my own presence on the web and, naturally, Google sends me alerts for everyone called Judith Morgan. The other Judith Morgan's online presence is still very active after her death. She was a writer and her books still sell well and attract mentions almost every day. She has left a legacy, whether or not that was her intention.

What sort of legacy do you want to leave? A big one, a small one, or somewhere in between?

If you are creating anything that has a life beyond you then it has the potential to go on without you. If you are an artist or a writer that might just happen anyway. After your death, your work might even become more valuable simply because you aren't creating any more.

If you have kids, you are leaving a legacy, you are leaving this planet in their tender care and in that of their progeny too.

There are many ways to crack this legacy nut, especially if you feel called to greatness.

If I look at my current clients, none of whom are hovering on the brink of death by the way, their websites, their photographs, their videos and podcasts, their impact on the lives of others will go on and on, as Celine would sing. And some are even creating businesses which will change hands, perhaps more than once, so if you are a starter and you've created something of value, you can pass it on to another owner/manager and it could, if you write it into the deal, make you and your loved ones a passive percentage in perpetuity. Nice alliteration, Judith!

It is highly likely that you have already made a life-changing difference to someone, perhaps even to a stranger without even knowing it. In fact, knowing you, I bet you have. The very act of you deciding to employ yourself for money will have encouraged another to at least think about it.

If you are a healer in any sense, then you are changing people's lives for the better every day and they take that home and are nicer to each other in their family and with their friends and colleagues. The ripples of what we do already spread outwards, farther than we can ever know.

I have a client whose work is all around helping others to create something of value which they may leave behind if that's important to them. And when I look at her journey throughout her career, where she's done that in business, this is the inevitable conclusion. If this is true for my client, it may also be true for you. Only you can make that decision. And the decision you make today might not serve you forever, you are always entitled to change your mind.

- How do you feel about legacy?
- Do you want to leave one?
- Do you know what it is yet?

PROFILES, ARCHETYPES AND LIMITING LABELS

When I was in my teens and twenties it was the Cosmo quiz. Who could resist answering those questions and discovering nonsense about yourself from your answers? Why, despite it being nonsense, did we go on participating in that malarkey? Because it was a diverting few minutes of fun.

Why do we do the silly quizzes on Facebook too, despite many of my FB friends complaining what's wrong with them even despite my frequent reminders that they are just a little bit of fun?

We are on an apparently endless quest to know ourselves, however silly the test.

And when it comes to employing ourselves for money this is no different. In fact, it may be worse.

My profiling system of choice is Wealth Dynamics*. I am a Creator*. You?

I quite like Myers Briggs too. I am an INFJ. You?

But there it ends. It is QUITE useful for me to know my client's Wealth Dynamics* profile as it helps us both to understand why they find some things harder or easier than others. And as Paul McKenna and Richard Bandler made me pledge to understand at the end of my NLP training, it is the road map, not The Way.

Don't be an eejit with this stuff, basically.

Don't hide behind it.

Don't restrict yourself by telling yourself that, of course, you can't do X because you are a Y.

It is just meaningless, and a meaninglessness from which we try to make meaning. Get a grip!

And don't start me on archetypes.

Honestly, if this stuff is fascinating to you, then fill your boots. But either use it in your work or just call it fun, like the Cosmo quiz.

Here's a blog post wot I wrote about this topic one day when I got rather cross about people using their profiles as an excuse not to get shiz done. Honestly, you may have a propensity towards some stuff and away from others, but you can do 100% of anything you put your mind to. https://www.judithmorgan.com/labels/

I hate video but even I can watch it when I want to learn the content enough, or when a couple of my clients do really lovely FB Lives.

I'm a podcaster but don't listen to much audio except Desert Island Discs and the funny news shows on BBC Radio 4.

I love the written word as a way of gathering information about anything and disseminating it too. But I know that people don't read as much as I do and therefore in choosing an emphasis on the written word, I will only reach those who love it as much as I do. And that's more than enough for me.

But, if push came to shove, I could watch and listen too. I just prefer to read.

Get it? Don't let this stuff convince you that you can't do something or anything. You can. Get a grip! Did I say that? Yes, get a grip. There's no hiding place. And pigeon-holing yourself is just a way of limiting your possibilities and your potential.

Don't let the labels limit you. Oh it looks like this rattles my cage so much I've written more than one blog post about it!

https://www.judithmorgan.com/how-do-you-let-your-labels-limit-you/

DO YOU HAVE (OR NEED) AN ELEVATOR PITCH?

My woo woo readers will not be surprised to learn that on the day when I decided I would write about this topic, not one but two clients asked me about elevator pitches. Coinkydink.

This was especially useful because there was a resource I knew I wanted to look up for you about this, and they gave me cause to do that.

So, to elevator pitches.

I HATE THEM!

They sound so forced and rehearsed and dull and formulaic. Please don't do that. Please don't be that.

Disclaimer: As already confessed, you know I don't go formal networking and yes, you are more likely to need one in those circumstances, but the same rules apply - no forced, rehearsed, dull or formulaic. Be your lovely natural self, even if that means you bungle it once or twice. Don't be a robot. Don't always play by the rules; make your own to the extent that a rule is even required.

Be memorable. Do it your way. Get across one or two tiny Marmite-y things so they can get an impression of you. You have such tiny amount of time in which to do that, you'd be better off saying nothing at all for most of the time. That'd get 'em on the edge of their seats.

All I want people to be able to do when they meet me or read about me or hear about me is to remember two things.

1. Judith
2. Coach

And then I want them to be able to go home and Google Judith coach and find me on the first page of the organic search results. End of.

Oh, and I don't have business cards either, for the same reason. I don't want to fit the expected norms. What's my name? Google it! That's how I want you to find me. That's my client, someone who wants the answer to everything without the necessity of leaving home unless they choose it.

Yes, when I was an accountant I had a business card. I saw the point. People would ask for them so they had all my contact details in one place, but that was then. And you may have that need now, but I do not. And after I'd thrown a few boxes away, I stopped printing them. These days I'd rather people either Googled me and emailed me from my website, or found me and befriended me on Facebook and PM'd me. It's the modern way in my business. And that's the point. What's the method you want to be using today in your business? Do that then.

Instead of an elevator pitch, I'd probably ask them something about themselves, they are more interested in that topic anyway. Make an impact. Dare to be different. Be memorable.

And yes, I know you need - or feel you do - an elevator pitch in more places than just formal networking.

The two clients who have asked me about it today are talking about how they describe themselves and their services online and the received wisdom reply to that is to have the copy for your various social media profiles filed somewhere where you can copy and paste it and ADAPT it to the new place where you are using it.

If you are writing it on your website, remember what I advised earlier, that every word can be changed every day if you want to.

You won't get this right at the beginning. No-one does. Change it to keep it fresh but don't change it endlessly and be a slippery eel as people won't be able to get a handle on who you are and what you do and how you help.

Make it as different, punchy, fun and unique as you are. Don't follow the rules. Look them up, then bend them to fit, to make them you-shaped.

Here's that resource I was telling you about. It is quite fun to give it a go and guess what? It might even help!

www.bettymeansbusiness.com/2013/05/29/how-to-explain-what-you-do/

WHAT'S YOUR BIGGEST PROBLEM?

My biggest problem is the dreadful survey question "what's your biggest problem...?" So cheesy, so lazy, so impossible to answer.

Don't do that.

In fact, don't do surveys. Everyone lies. The acid test is when you ask them for money. If they buy it today, tomorrow or in a few years' time, they like it. If they don't, it's back to the drawing board. And remember, no-one buys the first time you show it to them either. We've covered that. They'll pin it to the virtual cork board and watch while you make a go of it first before they eventually pile in. All except us early adopters, and we'll keep you going until then.

All sorts of experts and gurus will ask you to ask the audience. Don't. Look how well that works out on the talent shows. Don't ask the audience to do anything important unless you give them very strict guidelines and parameters and ignore them when they overstep that. Since almost no-one can follow the instructions, it's better not to do it at all. It is most unsettling at best. And can put you off entirely at worst. Don't, alright? Just don't.

You might as well get good as early as possible at making up your own mind about everything, 'cos when you ask other people guess what happens? You split the vote and you undermine your own confidence. You discover that everyone else has the full rainbow of opinions and how is that helpful? To my mind, I just see it as having the potential to unsettle you further. And I don't want that for you in any circumstances.

Yesterday a new client's brief to me was to make sure she keeps true to herself and to stop comparing herself to others. Music to my ears.

In the same vein, stop seeking approval, asking other people what they think, being swayed by the way they are doing it, feeling comparisonitis, paying any attention to friends and family who are probably not self-employed and, even if they are, are never going to be your clients anyway. Get used to asking yourself first. And even if you ask me I am likely to ask you "What do YOU think?" and we'll take it from there.

The whole point of this book you'll remember is learning to trust yourself. I already trust you. You seem to have lost your way a bit on that from time to time. Let's get you back there a.s.a.p. Your own wisdom is best. Relax, you've got this.

ROLL OF HONOUR

Thank you to everyone who submitted thoughts and topics and questions, or a series of them, specifically with this book in mind.

Honourable mention must go to Claire Maycock, Gillian Lancaster and Lotte Lane who surpassed themselves both in the number of useful questions they sent to me and in the bonkersness factor. I love you three especially for your support in this way and I know you ask your Qs and offer me your bonkersness on behalf of those who are less brave and less happy to have their navel gazed at quite so publicly in this book. You are rock stars, I am not sure where I should have been without you this summer, my first as an author.

Special mention goes to those who sent in a cracking question or two including Louise Taylor, Anne Walsh and Andrea Jordan. You all made the cut. Thank you too, you Top Birds.

All current clients and past ones too are reflected somehow in this, my first proper book. Those who very much came to mind when I was writing include (but are not limited to) Sarah, Stephanie, Robin, Jayne, Richard, Liz, Alison, Charlotte, Julia, the other Liz, Joanna, Heena, Justina and Tracy. You are loved and respected, more than mere words can say.

And to everyone I work with in my PWYW sessions, Small Business Big Magic and Club 100, thank you for your forbearance while I was off writing Your Biz Your Life. You are my inspiration in this book, as you are every week in my newsy newsletter too.

If I have offended any client or reader by my trademark razor sharp and blunt, then I apologise unreservedly. I think you know that is never my intention, but Michael Neill taught me that it is a brave coach who holds up the mirror.

I hold up mine for you, my lovely clients and readers. And my mirror is, as you can imagine, a pretty pink one. I try at all times to make sure that my own reflection in that same mirror is as true as it can be, given our humanity.

Gillian's website: https://relaxandcreate.today/
Read more about Anne: http://www.the-excel-expert.com/
And here's Lotte: http://www.lottelane.com/
This is Andrea: http://learndiscoverbefree.com
Claire's online home is: http://www.clairemaycock.com/
Look! It's Louise: http://www.shoutthesun.co.uk/

WHAT NEXT?

Join Ask Judith and ask your question for free and get my opinionated personal answer on Facebook in our Closed Group: www.22s.com/judith/askjudith

Want to do that privately? Book a Pay What You Want session and make a donation via PayPal at: https://www.judithmorgan.com/PWYW

Become a client of Small Business Big Magic and work with me on all these issues in your own business and life at: https://www.judithmorgan.com/small-business-big-magic £750 per annum.

LET'S KEEP IN TOUCH!

Read my weekly newsy newsletter published at 10 a.m. UK time every Friday without fail. Just pop your name and email in here http://eepurl.com/czmctD

Listen to our weekly podcast Own It! Your Business AND Your Life at: http://ownitthepodcast.com/ or subscribe via iTunes or Stitcher and you can do that via the links at the bottom of each show on our podcast website

Email me: https://www.judithmorgan.com/contact - send me your question for next year's YBYW book 2018

Follow me on Twitter https://twitter.com/judithmorgan - let's tweet

Like my Facebook Page https://www.facebook.com/TheSmallBusinessOracle/ and message me to say Hi and tell me about how you found the book

Hit me up with a Friend request Facebook https://www.facebook.com/judith.morgan1

ACKNOWLEDGEMENTS

Thank you to my 3-woman proofreading tag team of kind and supportive pals Jo Dodds, Liz Truckle and Marion Ryan.

To photographer Alison Read: http://alisonread.co.uk/ who took my photos for the book.

And makeup artist Marzi: https://www.facebook.com/AshfordNails/ who did the makeup for the photos.

#Wonderwomen

Printed in Great Britain
by Amazon